SAMUEL LOGAN BRENGLE

Heart for God

Foreword by General Eva Burrows AC (Rtd)

Edited by Peter Farthing

CARPENTER MEDIA
PO Box A435, Sydney South 1235, Australia

© The Salvation Army 2009 All rights reserved.

Printed in Australia
ISBN 978-0-9807410-0-1

Carpenter Media is an arm of The Salvation Army
Australia Eastern Territory   61-2-92641711

Cover design by Kem Pobjie
Printed by SOS Print and Media, Alexandria NSW, Australia

Contents

Christian life

Christian Service

Spiritual Formation Small Group Notes

Foreword

Samuel Logan Brengle is a household name in Salvation Army circles; he is revered as our apostle of holiness who preached it, wrote it and embodied it in truth, as he nurtured the spiritual life of The Salvation Army over many decades. He is often quoted widely from his many practical books on the subject; however in this day and age he is infrequently read. A great pity. But the often ponderous Victorian English, the convoluted sentences and archaic vocabulary of Brengle's era have often deterred younger readers. But now, Peter Farthing has had the courage to 'paraphrase' these timeless words into contemporary language, and we hear Brengle speak with a modern accent that comes across with a startling relevance

So I congratulate the author on this book which introduces us gently to the Brengle writings and presents a fresh look at the deep and often radical things he had to say about holy living. God designed us for holiness; it relates to the totality of life. Therefore the passages in this book, chosen from 9 of Brengle's volumes, capture his thoughts on the empowering and purifying, lifelong work of the Holy Spirit within us. They will keep you 'in step with the Holy Spirit', and you will sense Brengle's wisdom, his understanding of human nature, his sympathy with our failings, his awareness of our yearnings and hopes. He doesn't write like a theologian, but like a spiritual counselor and friend. If it's your first time to read Brengle, you will be delighted and challenged.

Let me encourage you to explore these extracts selected on the key aspects of: Christian Essentials, Christian Holiness, Christian Life and Christian Service. They will expand your thinking, and correct the idea that many people have had that holiness is exclusively personal. Here it places the believer at the disposal of God for the service of others.

On many an occasion when a person spoke to Brengle about the powerful effects of his preaching, he would humbly say , 'But it is not me. I just stand back and watch God at work.' As you read these pages from his pen, they will resonate in your heart and mind, and you will also sense that God is at work in you.

General Eva Burrows AC (Rtd)

Introduction

'It is a good rule after reading a new book,' advised CS Lewis of *Narnia* fame, 'never to allow yourself another new one till you have read an old one in between.' So here is an old book—in fact readings from 9 books written by one of The Salvation Army's finest authors.

Not incredibly old, I should add. Samuel Logan Brengle died the same year the BBC broadcast its first television service—1936. There is a recording of him speaking, and at least once he was involved in a car accident. So his era was not so far removed from ours.

Brengle was a Salvation Army officer, and an internationally famous Christian teacher. More than that—he was a holiness teacher. All around the world people read his books and came to hear him preach. Translated into many languages, his books sold over a million copies and have remained in print to this day. General John Larsson judged that 'no one outside the Booth family itself made a greater spiritual impact on The Salvation Army' than Brengle. Thousands of ministers and lay people in other churches also thanked God for him.

Although well educated theologically, Brengle did not write for theologians. As General Fred Coutts remarked, Brengle, 'has the human touch. Perhaps his secret is that he wrote from his heart to the needs of the human heart.' He had a pastoral style, and after reading *Heart for God* for a while, I suspect you will feel Brengle is talking to you.

His is a voice worth hearing. It is true that, like every great Christian, Brengle was shaped by his times. He absorbed certain theological ideas which do not always travel well today. But if we leave aside that theological system—as I have done in this book—there remains in Brengle's writing a hefty load of biblical and practical teaching. We can summarise Brengle's insights on Christian holiness with three principles:

1.   God wants the Christian to dedicate his whole person to him, mind, heart and will. He wants us to break with all known sin, to step down from pride and ambition.

2. God wants to clean us from the damaging influence of sin—he does not expect us to thrash about in the shallows of Christianity forever, constantly defeated.

3. God wants to fill our lives with his Spirit—the Spirit of love.

It would be a pity if The Salvation Army ever forgot Samuel Logan Brengle or reduced his name to a point of theological debate. No people—no nation or movement or sport or church—can afford to despise its heroes. If America needs Ben Franklin, and nursing needs Florence Nightingale, and science needs Isaac Newton, then The Salvation Army needs Samuel Logan Brengle. We do not have to agree with every word he spoke, any more than today's physicists think Newton had the last word. However we do need to respect his enormous influence under God.

In *Heart for God* you will be reading Brengle in modernised language. Writers in his day could be wordy. Like Victorian furniture, their sentences wore a lot of ornamentation and flourish. I have pared Brengle down to a more modern style. In parts, this is almost a paraphrase— you might say, *The Message* version of Brengle. Is it right to do this? I reason Brengle was a communicator, and communicators want to communicate. He didn't write for the ages, he wrote to help; in fact most of his chapters originally appeared in weekly Salvation Army magazines. So I don't think he would mind us modernising his sentences.

Brengle was a humble man. In 1886 he was studying for the ministry at Boston University's School of Theology when he heard William Booth preach in Tremont Temple Baptist Church in downtown Boston. Booth impressed him tremendously, especially with his vision for bringing salvation to the poor. Not long after, Brengle met and eventually married Elizabeth Swift, an educated young woman who had met and joined the Army while on holidays in Britain. In time Samuel Logan Brengle felt called to leave his prospects for large churches, and become a Salvationist.

It was a struggle. Brengle had a good education and excellent prospects, and many Army congregations were small and in needy communities. But Brengle heard a call to teach those people, to explain especially how God could make them holy. Two weeks into his training in London he wrote home: 'I don't know yet, of course, what kind of a little place the Lord has for us in the Army, but I feel that my work will be particularly to promote holiness.'

After training he became a local corps officer or pastor back in the USA. One night a drunken thug threw a brick which hit Brengle in the head and almost killed him. Brengle was off work, in bed, for 18 months. But thankfully, during his period of recovery, he began to write articles, and they turned into his first book, *Helps to Holiness*. Brengle later said, 'If there had been no brick there would have been no books.'

In time he recovered enough to preach as well, and eventually became a full-time travelling preacher, first in the USA, and then for the whole world.

In 1907 Brengle arrived in Norway where two movements were sweeping the churches—one was a renewal movement which emphasised speaking in tongues, and the other was a movement called New Theology which doubted the miraculous and could deny truths such as the divinity of Christ. Brengle's approach to tongues was to teach the Bible, especially emphasising practical holiness. When he arrived in the city of Bergen he found he was to address a large crowd on the New Theology. Brengle was not one for disputes, but he wanted to touch hearts with the truth at the heart of the Gospel.

On the night of the meeting, he entered the hall and saw a great crowd of church leaders, professors, lawyers, journalists. Taking his seat on the platform he nervously looked down at the used envelope on which he had found time to write down a few notes. When he got to his feet all fear vanished.

'God came upon me,' he recalled. 'I never felt his presence with me more. My mind worked with perfect clarity. I seemed clothed with the Holy Spirit.'

Others thought so too. People sat up straight, straining to see and hear him as he expounded the great theme, the Atonement. 'Before them they saw a man terribly alive and on fire. Reporters from the local press started to take notes, then put down their pencils. Beside Brengle on the platform stood Adjutant Theodore Westegaard, who was acting as translator. Westergaard would interpret a sentence, throw it out to the audience, then whisper between his translations: 'Beautiful! Give it to them, Colonel!' (Clarence Hall).

When he finished, people crowded forward to shake his hand. A publisher asked for the manuscript to print, but Brengle had only the envelope. One man who later became an evangelist, wrote, 'I have heard hundreds of preachers but I never heard anything like the Atonement address. It was the most remarkable testimony to the divinity of Christ I have ever heard. Something was fixed that day in my soul. My own doubts flew away. I knew my Lord was divine and I have known it ever since.'

What we see in that incident is a man filled and shaped

and powered by the Spirit of God.

Brengle was a man of God, and consequently a remarkably good man. When, in a book on Christ, the great Anglican Bible teacher John Stott gave examples of Christ-likeness, he told a story about Brengle. Young people gravitated to him. Needy people sought his help. Men and women around the world wrote letters, and received counsel in return. People trusted Samuel Logan Brengle.

I hope you enjoy his wise counsel and teaching.

Samuel Logan Brengle

What is holiness?

A number of years ago a girl in her teens asked me, 'What is this sanctification, or holiness?'

She had heard it preached about for nearly a year, so her question surprised and almost discouraged me. But I rallied, and asked, 'Have you a bad temper?'

'Yes,' she said, 'I have a temper like a volcano.'

'Sanctification,' I replied, 'is to have that bad temper taken out.'

That definition set her thinking, but it was too narrow. If I had said, 'Sanctification is to have temper and all sin taken away, and the heart filled with love to God and man,' that would have done, for that is sanctification. That is holiness. It is, in our measure, to be made like God. It is to be made a 'participant of the Divine nature' (2 Peter 1:4).

A spark from the fire is like the fire. The tiniest twig on the giant oak has the nature of the oak and is in that respect like the oak. A drop of water on the end of your finger from the ocean is like the ocean: not in its size, of course, but it is like the ocean in its character, in its nature. Similarly, a holy person is like God. Not that he is infinite as God is; he does not know everything; he has not all power and wisdom as God has; but he is like God in his nature. He is good and pure, and loving and just, in the same way that God is.

Holiness, then, is conformity to the nature of God. It is likeness to God, as he is revealed in Jesus.

(*The Way of Holiness*)

Why should you be holy?

Why should you be holy? Why is it such an important subject? Why do we talk about holiness so often? Does it really have to become a feature of my life?

1. We should be holy because God wants us to be holy. He commands it. The Bible says, 'let yourselves be pulled into a way of life shaped by God's life, a life energetic and blazing with holiness. God said, "I am holy; you be holy"' (1 Peter 1:15 *TM*). God is serious about this. It is God's will, and it cannot be evaded. Just as a man wants his watch to keep time, his friends to be loyal and his wife to be faithful, so God wants us to be holy.

Does this seem hard to you? Many people have suffered harsh words and blows in life, so this may seem hard. But we must not forget that 'God is love,' and his commands are not harsh, but kind. They come from an infinitely loving and all-wise heart. They are meant for our good.

The person who refuses to obey God's commands to be holy, ultimately hurts himself. God wants what is best for us. Listen to his command to Israel: 'So now, O Israel, what does the Lord your God require of you? Only to fear the Lord your God, to walk in all his ways, to love him, to serve the Lord your God with all your heart and with all your soul, and to keep the commandments of the Lord your God, and his decrees that I am commanding you today, for your own well-being (Deuteronomy 10:12,13 *NRSV*). Notice—'for your own well-being.' Holiness is good for you.

2. We should be holy, because Jesus died to make us holy. He gave himself to beatings and cruel mocking and the crown of thorns and death on the cross for this purpose. As he was preparing for the Cross, Jesus prayed for his disciples: 'Sanctify them by the truth; your word is truth.' (John 17:17.) Holiness was on his mind. Paul says, 'Christ loved the church. He gave up his life for her to make her holy and clean' (Ephesians 5:25 *NLT*).

3. We should be holy, in order that we may be useful. Who have been the mightiest men of God of all the ages? The holy men; men with clean hearts on fire with love to God and man; unselfish men; humble men, who forgot themselves in their love and work for others; faithful men, whose lives were 'hid with Christ in God' (Colossians 3:3). Moses, humble before God, Paul, servant of God and the Gospel, Martin Luther, Saint Francis of Assisi, William and Catherine Booth—those were holy people God used.

For these three, and for other reasons as well, we ought to go to God and ask him to make our lives holy.

(The Way of Holiness)

Spiritual breakthrough

On January 9, 1885, at about nine o'clock in the morning, God sanctified my soul. I was in my own room at the time, but in a few minutes I went out and met a man and told him what God had done for me. The next morning, I met another friend on the street and told him the story. He praised God and urged me to preach full salvation. God used him to encourage and help me. So the following day I preached on the subject as clearly and forcibly as I could, and ended with my testimony.

God blessed the word mightily to others, but I think he blessed it most to myself. That confession put me on record. It cut the bridges down behind me. I could not go back now.

So two mornings after that, just as I got out of bed and

was reading some of the words of Jesus, he gave me such a blessing as I never had dreamed a man could have this side of Heaven. *It was a heaven of love that came into my heart.* I walked out over Boston Common before breakfast weeping for joy and praising God. Oh, how I loved! In that hour I knew Jesus and I loved him till it seemed my heart would break with love. I loved the sparrows, I loved the dogs, I loved the horses, I loved the little urchins on the streets, I loved the strangers who hurried past me, I loved the heathen—I loved the whole world.

Do you want to know what holiness is? It is pure love.

Do you want to know what it is to be filled by the Holy Spirit? It is not a mere emotion. It is an infusion of love that brings every thought into captivity to the Lord Jesus (2 Corinthians 10:5); that drives out all fear (1 John 4:18); that burns up doubt and unbelief; that makes one 'gentle and humble in heart' (Matthew 11:29); that makes one hate uncleanness, lying and deceit, a flattering tongue and every evil way with a perfect hatred; that makes Heaven and Hell eternal realities; that makes one patient and gentle with the obstinate and sinful; that makes one 'pure . . . peace-loving, considerate, submissive, full of mercy and good fruit, impartial and sincere' (James 3:17); that brings one into perfect and unbroken sympathy with the Lord Jesus Christ in his effort to bring a lost and rebel world back to God.

God did all that for me, bless his holy name!

(Helps to Holiness)

Missing Jesus

I remember a number of years ago going to a convention hoping to find Jesus there in power. I got there two or three days after the opening, and I found, if I now remember rightly, that no one had been saved. There was no grip and power in the meetings. They would begin with a rush, and songs and prayers and jokes and laughter and collection and testimonies and a Bible reading would follow, and the meeting would end again without souls finding God. Everybody would go out good-naturedly, make a rush for the best seats at the dinner-table, and enjoy themselves until the next meeting.

Everyone seemed to take it for granted that Jesus was in the gathering, yet no one seemed to be especially conscious of his presence.

When Jesus was a boy of 12, he went with his parents

and neighbours up to Jerusalem to the Feast of the Passover. 'After the Feast was over, while his parents were returning home, the boy Jesus stayed behind in Jerusalem, but they were unaware of it. Thinking he was in their company, they travelled on for a day. Then they began looking for him among their relatives and friends. When they did not find him, they went back to Jerusalem to look for him' (Luke 2:43-45). Their mistake was in taking it for granted that Jesus was in the company. Joseph knew he was not with him, and Mary knew he was not with her, and their relatives and friends knew he was not with them, and yet each took it for granted that he was with someone else. But when they searched for him, they could not find him. He was not there.

Convention

At last it was pointed out that the conference meetings were galloped through but no souls were saved. And it was suggested that perhaps Jesus was missing. A prayer meeting was called to look for Jesus, and some of the people present had to admit that Jesus was not with them. Then some of them went to their rooms to look for Jesus, and some went to the woods and got down on their knees to look for him, and would not give up the search until at last—praise him—he was found. And when he was told that he was expected and that he must come, and that we would not let him go except he blessed us, then he came.

The Christians got awfully focused, and the lost people got awfully convicted, so that they were no longer anxious about what they should have for dinner.

I tell you, it was wonderful, the transformation that came over that camp ground when Jesus got there! The shallow joy that put smiles on faces and made an empty racket, gave way before the deep joy of the Lord.

Now friends, let me promise you this. Jesus is ready and willing to go up to every convention and meeting all over the world, and to make his personal presence felt by every saint and soldier. But each one must look for him.

Jesus is holy and humble and he can only walk with humble, holy people. So if you want him to go with you, you must humble yourself and be holy. You must wait for him, and ask him to come.

If we want to know the presence of Jesus with us when we go home, he will not come if we close the door in his face, and go in and scold the wife and children and talk about our neighbours and forget who we are in Christ. Our walk with him must be constant, not irregular.

We need to always know he is with us. We go on a fool's errand if we go serving without his powerful presence. Poor Joseph and Mary lost five days and had much anxiety and heartache, all because they supposed Jesus was in the company, but did not make sure. Is he with you now? If he is not, then get your Bible and go off alone and seek him, and if you search for him with all your heart, you will find him.

(*Heart Talks on Holiness*)

The secret of power

If I was dying, and had the privilege of delivering three words to Christians, I would say, 'Wait for God!' Take time. Miss your breakfast if necessary, but take time to wait for God.

I once heard William Booth say in a Salvation Army officer's council: 'Take time to pray God's blessing down on your own soul every day. If you don't, you will lose God. God is leaving men every day. They once had power. They walked in the glory and strength of God, but they ceased to wait on him. They neglected to seek his face, and he left them. I am a very busy man, but I take time to get alone with God every day and commune with him.'

Wherever I go I find men and women who were once believers but have slid away. My heart aches as I think of the way in which the Holy Spirit has been grieved, and of the way in which Jesus has been treated.

If these backsliders were asked why they lost faith, they would give a thousand different reasons, but in the end there is really only one: they did not wait for God. If they had waited for him when the assault was made on their faith, they would have renewed their strength. They would have run through their enemies and not been weary. They would have walked in the middle of trouble and not fainted.

Wait for God.

This means more than a prayer of 30 seconds on getting up in the morning and going to bed at night. It may mean one prayer that gets hold of God and comes away with the blessing, or it may mean a dozen prayers that knock and persist and will not be put off, until God reveals his presence.

There is a drawing near to God, a knocking at Heaven's doors, a pleading of the promises, a reasoning with Jesus, that puts all the wealth of Heaven at the disposal of a person. Wait for God.

(*Helps to Holiness*)

Christian Essentials

Misrepresenting God

I read recently of a speaker who preached on the mercy of God, 'until it seemed there was nothing in God but mercy.' I fear he misrepresented God. Some religious teachers misrepresent God by making him angry and cruel; they gloat over Hell as if God cannot wait to send people there. Others represent God as a sort of goody-goody God, who fawns over sinners, and looks at worldly, superficial Christians with sentimental pity. Nothing could be further from the truth.

When we read the Bible we find God rebuked people who were living in rebellion against him. When Israel sinned, God spoke stern words:

Why bother reciting my decrees

and pretending to obey my covenant?

For you refuse my discipline

and treat my words like trash . . .

While you did all this, I remained silent

and you thought I didn't care.

But now I will rebuke you,

listing all my charges against you.

Repent, all of you who forget me'

(Psalm 50:16-22 *NLT*).

The truth lies between extremes. There is mercy in God, but it is mingled with severity. There is wrath in God, but it is tempered with mercy.

Fire will not only bake our food, but will also burn us. Water will not only quench our thirst, but may drown us. God's love will nurture us, but if we break God's laws and violate his ways, that love is bound to react. It is not a weak, wishy-washy love; it is a burning fire of love which cares passionately about right and goodness.

We must not deny the reality of God's wrath. Early in his letter to the Romans, Paul celebrated the Good News: 'it is the power of God for the salvation of everyone who believes.' But then he added: 'The wrath of God is being revealed from heaven against all the godlessness and wickedness of men who suppress the truth by their wickedness' (Romans 1:16-18.)

Later in the same letter, he warned: 'because you are stubborn and refuse to turn from your sin, you are storing up terrible punishment for yourself. For a day of anger is coming, when God's righteous judgment will be revealed' (Romans 2:5 *NLT*).

Therefore, although we must tell people about the love of God, we must not distort the message by neglecting to warn them of God's judgment and wrath. Tell them about judgment, and tell them God came and died in Christ the Son to save them from that judgment.

(*Love Slaves*)

The Atonement (Part 1)

No other subject is so vital as the atonement. That is, the work of our Lord Jesus Christ in suffering and dying for humanity to save them from sin. No other teaching does us more good.

So where do we begin? Right at the start we are face to face with the great problem of sin. If there is no sin, no estrangement from God, then there is no need for atonement. So let's begin with sin.

What is sin?

Is it a mild malady or a malignant cancer? I once stepped off the train at home and was told that my boy had the measles. I was not alarmed, and he soon recovered. But later I visited a leper hospital, and it was tragic. Sin is something that corresponds not to measles, but to leprosy.

Do not underestimate sin. In our sheltered Christian homes, and under the protection of laws framed in the light of 20 Christian centuries, we are apt to forget the malignant character of sin. We can be ignorant of human wickedness, of how bad people can be. There are men and women, possibly in your street, who would not hesitate to rob you, if they could. They would not hesitate a moment to malign your reputation, or seduce your sister.

What is sin?

We understand sin is an act. It is something we do—or something we ought to do which we do not do. But sin is not merely an act. It is a state of the heart as well.

Picture Jesus in Pilate's judgment hall. They have spat in his face, and crowned him with thorns, and stripped him, and beaten his back. He struggles up the hill under the heavy load. He is the very essence of humility. But you come strutting behind him in pride—proud of your clothes, your looks, your money in the bank, your home, your good name, gifts you possess. Your pride is sin of the heart.

Jesus calls out from the Cross, 'Father, forgive them; for they don't know what they are doing!' And you stand at the foot of the Cross, and some man or woman approaches you, and you frown and step aside, because you are angry with them. Your anger is a sin of the heart.

Sin is a wrong against God. It is a blow against God and his righteous government. David stole the wife of Uriah the Hittite and arranged the murder of Uriah. When he was convicted by the story told by Nathan, David saw that he had sinned against God. He called out, 'I have sinned against the LORD.'

Hundreds of years before, Joseph had been tempted to commit a similar sin. He resisted and overcame the temptation, saying, 'How then could I do such a wicked thing and sin against God?' (Genesis 39:9).

Do you remember the way Jesus described Judgment Day? The King will say to some of us, 'I was hungry and you did not feed me, I was homeless and you gave me no shelter' (Matthew 25:43). The King so identifies himself with the needy that when they are neglected, he is neglected. He feels it.

When a man sins, it is against God.

So then, we begin to see what a massive, tragic problem sin presents to the holy God. He is perfect, but sin is wrong actions—deeds, words, thoughts. God is good, but sin is wrong lodged in the human heart. God is love, but sin is rebellion against him and his love.

(*The Guest of the Soul*)

The Atonement (Part 2)

What is God's attitude to human sin? If sin is an endemic sickness of the human heart, which manifests itself in wrong actions and the failure to do right actions, how does God respond to it? Here are four simple truths:

1. God cannot be ignorant of sin.

2. God cannot be indifferent to sin.

3. God cannot approve of sin.

4. God must be utterly antagonistic to sin, with all the strength of his moral being. He must hate and condemn it.

On occasion you will read in the newspaper about some rotten crime—perhaps against a child. And you will burn with indignation. If a man or woman feels that way in the presence of sin, how do you think a holy God must feel?

If God does not hate sin he is not holy. If he does not condemn sin he is not righteous. If he is not prepared to punish sin he is not just. But God is holy, he is righteous, he is just. His great heart demands, and his holiness calls for, the utter condemnation of sin.

But God is also love. And while his holiness demands the punishment and utter destruction of sin, his heart of love calls for the salvation of the sinner.

Sin: a problem for God

So then, this was the situation with humanity which God faced. His holiness left only one option for sin—judgement. His love compelled him to find another option for people.

How could God accomplish this double and seemingly contradictory demand of his holy and loving heart? How could God's love and holiness harmonise to secure mercy for the sinner and judgment against the sin?

How can God be just, and yet justify the ungodly? How can God see sin and make an ungodly man right, and yet be a holy God? If a judge on the bench is careless in the way he deals with criminals, he is a dangerous man. That judge is a dangerous character if he does not watch over the interests of society and deal with wrong-doing. And is it not exactly the same with God?

Here is a problem for God. Foolish men and women think it is a very simple problem, this matter of the forgiveness of sins; but it is the profoundest problem in the moral universe.

Sin: How can God forgive it?

How then can God forgive sin and be holy? Here are a further three great truths.

1.   God must secure repentance in the sinner, or the person he forgives will only be hardened in sin.

2.   God must make wrong-doers know that they cannot sin with impunity.

3.   God must safeguard his moral universe. He must make everyone feel the holiness of the law and the righteousness of his judgments, so they say, 'Just and true are your ways, King of the ages' (Revelation 15:3). 'Yes, Lord God Almighty, true and just are your judgments' (Revelation 16:7).

(*The Guest of the Soul*)

The Atonement (Part 3)

God was faced with an awful cosmic dilemma which involved every man, woman and child on this earth. He resolved that terrible dilemma by sending his Son, Jesus the Christ, to die on the Cross. The judgment of sin was carried out—on the Son of God himself.

That Sufferer hanging there was God, suffering for us—God the blessed Son. 'God was reconciling the world to himself in Christ' (2 Corinthians 5:19). 'And being found in appearance as a man, he humbled himself and became obedient to death—even death on a cross!' (Philippians 2:8). 'God made him who had no sin to be sin for us, so that in him we might become the righteousness of God' (2 Corinthians 5:21). It was 'through the eternal Spirit (Christ) offered himself unblemished to God' (Hebrews 9:14), on our behalf.

Do not imagine that somehow a loving Son gave himself to appease an angry Father. That is not correct. The whole Trinity is involved in the atoning work of Jesus Christ on Calvary. The Father 'so loved the world that he gave his one and only Son' (John 3:16).

The Father's heart was pierced by the thorns that pierced the head of the Son. The Father's heart was hurt with the nails that pierced the hands and feet of the Son. The Father suffered with and in the blessed Son.

Our response

This is the atonement—God's act of mercy, which bridges the gulf between sinful humanity and the holy God.

The atonement makes God right in all his ways with sinful men. The holiest beings in the universe can never feel that God is indifferent to sin, when he pardons a believing sinner, because Christ has died for him. On the other hand, the sinner who is lost and banished to outer darkness, cannot blame God or charge him with indifference, since Christ, by tasting death for him, flung wide open the gateway of escape.

The atonement opens wide the door of pardon, of salvation to every penitent sinner who will trust Christ and follow him. At the same time, it sweeps away every excuse from the impenitent sinner who will not trust and obey him.

I once heard General William Booth, Founder of The Salvation Army, in the middle of an impassioned appeal to men to repent and make their peace with God, call out, 'Every sinner must be either pardoned or punished.' And, ever since, these words have remained in my memory as the expression of a tremendous truth from which there is no escape.

God wants to pardon you—he wants to pardon every person. Remember: the atonement opens wide the door of pardon and forgiveness.

(*The Guest of the Soul*)

Wishing for a more 'powerful' Christ

Some Christians wish God would show his hand and prove to 'all those heathens' he is King. They become discouraged by the Gospel's apparent slow progress. They are distressed to see evil flourishing in this world. So they wish Christ would return, overthrow his enemies, and see every knee bow before him.

But that is not how God wins hearts. That is not how he conquers. He conquers through the Cross.

One day he will come in power, but it will not be to change the hearts of men—not then, it will be too late. He will come to judge.

But until that day, the spectacular overwhelming display of power is not God's way with his world. Jesus forever gave up the spectacular way when he refused to throw himself down from the pinnacle of the Temple at Satan's suggestion. Instead he chose the humble, painful way of loving sacrifice. Only through his Cross will he 'reconcile to himself all things' (Colossians 1:20).

So what do we say to those who wish for a more 'powerful' Christ? What do we say to people who want him to overpower evil in our world? If God interfered to prevent sin by some flaming spectacle of power and glory, this would ignore and destroy the freedom of the human will. If God forced us into goodness, then we would become good machines, not good men.

What, then, does God do to overcome man's sin? God leaves the freedom of man's will untouched. He presents to that will, at great cost to himself, a different way. Christ reaches out to the free man and waits in love.

God does not want reluctant, resentful subjects; he wants penitent sons and daughters. He wants hearts broken, and open to his love. You cannot change a heart by force, you have to use love. And that is God's way.

(*Resurrection Life and Power*)

Resurrection power

I want you to try to feel the hopelessness of the disciples as they fell asleep on the Saturday after Good Friday. Their faces were heavy after crying; they felt drained. With the death of Christ, their hopes also died. When the tortured Jesus spoke his last words from the Cross, their faith suffered a total eclipse.

Those men had been through such a terrible turnaround. Three years before, the disciples left everything to follow him. They heard his matchless teaching, saw his miracles, felt his compassion. They expected to see him at any time overthrow the Romans and ascend the throne of David. So sure were they, that they wrangled amongst themselves as to who should be the greatest in this kingdom.

Jesus had warned them. He explained that he would be rejected and killed, but that he would rise again. But they did not understand this, they did not believe. Peter said, 'This will never happen to you!' (Matthew 16:22).

When they arrived in Jerusalem for the Passover, an immense crowd cut palm branches and waved them, calling out, 'Hosanna to the Son of David!' (Matthew 21:9). It must have been a tremendous moment for the disciples.

But soon, instead of ascending a throne, Jesus was hung on a cross. Yes, he did wear a crown, but it was a crown of thorns. Like a king, he did have a man on either side, but they were not attendants—they were crucified thieves. He was coming into his kingdom, but it was by the gate of death. This was his glory.

How could the disciples understand all this? Well, they did not understand, and when he died, their hopes died too.

They forgot he had said he would rise again. It is strange that they should forget such a startling statement; but they did. But, thankfully, God does not depend on our ability to remember his promises!

Jesus Christ rose just as he said he would. The grave could not hold the prince of life. He broke its bars. He scattered its darkness. He conquered its terrors. He robbed it of its victory. 'Where O death, is your victory?

Where, O death, is your sting?' (1 Corinthians 15:55).

The disciples saw him. He made them to know that it was him; 'gave many convincing proofs' (Acts 1:3). Once again they looked into those eyes of infinite compassion. Once more they listened to his voice and heard him teach.

'Praise be to the God and Father of our Lord Jesus Christ!' Peter would later write. 'In his great mercy he has given us new birth into a living hope through the resurrection of Jesus Christ from the dead' (1 Peter 1:3).

(*Resurrection Life and Power*)

The significance of the resurrection

The resurrection changed everything for the disciples. And we know it remains crucially important; we sing about it and celebrate it every Easter and mention it in our prayers. But what did the resurrection of Jesus really mean for the disciples? What did Christ's resurrection achieve? What is its significance for today?

1. The resurrection was God's complete vindication of Jesus as the Christ of God.

How do we know for sure that Jesus was the Christ, the Son of God? How did the disciples know? Even John the Baptist grew uncertain at one stage and sent messengers to ask Jesus, 'Are you the one who was to come, or should we expect someone else?' (Matthew

11:3). But the resurrection was God's complete answer. As Paul declared (in a complex but wonderful sentence), the crucified Jesus was 'declared with power to be the Son of God by his resurrection from the dead' (Romans 1:4). 'His unique identity as Son of God was shown by the Spirit when Jesus was raised from the dead, setting him apart as the Messiah, our Master' (Romans 1:4 *TM*).

2. The resurrection was God's evidence that Christ had atoned for the sins of the world.

The resurrection was God's vindication of Jesus. Christ came through. He conquered. The victory had been won. Man was reconciled to God. The price had been paid so all people could be made right with God (justified) through his grace. And God the Father proved all of that when he raised the Son to life.

3. The resurrection gives hope for life beyond death.

'Christ has been raised to life! And he makes us certain that others will also be raised to life' (1 Corinthians 15:20 *CEV*). He led the way! In the presence of the risen Jesus we can confidently say death does not end all. There is life beyond the grave.

Our loved ones die, but believers do not mourn like

those who have no hope. The people we love are 'absent from the body, but present with the Lord' (2 Corinthians 5:8). They are with Jesus, and they see his face (Revelation 22:4).

4. Christ's resurrection provides *life* to you now.

The apostles worked tirelessly to help people see that now, while they were still in this life, they could enter into the resurrection power of Jesus. They could walk with him with new life (Romans 6:4).

Paul says we are reconciled to God by the death of Jesus, but we are saved by his life (Romans 5:10). You see he does not only provide pardon for our past, he brings new life and power for our present. That is, resurrection life. We can die to sin and live the life of Heaven here upon earth, filled with a constant sense of the favour of God, having power to overcome sin, and to do the will of God on earth as it is done in Heaven.

A brilliant young minister came to one of my holiness meetings and later asked to talk with me. He told me what an awful struggle he was having with temptations, so much so that he would walk the streets almost in agony. He had been reconciled to God by the death of Jesus, but he had not yet learned that he was also saved by his life. But after having the way explained to him he began to give himself to that resurrection power Christ had brought into his life. He asked God to fill him. And God did. After that, the minister began to truly walk with new life.

So then, that is why the resurrection is so significant. First, it was God's complete vindication of Jesus Christ as the Son of God. Second, it is God's evidence that Christ atoned for the sins of the world. Third, it is God's victory over death—and therefore it gives hope for us beyond our final breath. And fourth, the resurrection releases life for now, for all who will trust in Christ.

(*Resurrection Life and Power*)

Witnesses to the resurrection

Several years ago, I knelt in prayer with a young woman who wanted to be holy. I asked her if she would give up everything for Jesus. She answered that she would. I then thought I would put a hard test to her, and asked her if she would be willing to go to Africa as a missionary for Jesus. She said, 'Yes.' Then we prayed, and while we were praying, she burst into tears and said emphatically, 'O Jesus!'

She had never seen Jesus. She had never heard his voice. But she knew him! This young woman was a witness of Jesus—a witness that he is not dead but living, and as such she was a witness to his resurrection.

There are two kinds of evidence for the resurrected Christ, each of which seems to be necessary to get men to accept the truth and be saved. First, there is the evidence we get from history—from the Bible. Second, there is the evidence of living men and women.

I remember a girl in Boston, who would give a quiet, thoughtful testimony for Jesus, which touched people. One day, as we were walking along the street, she said to me: 'The other evening, as I was in my room getting ready for the meeting, Jesus was with me. I felt he was there, and I knew him.'

I replied, 'We may be more conscious of his presence than of any earthly friend.'

Then, to my surprise, she said, 'Yes, because he is in our hearts.' She was a witness. And you can be a witness to the resurrection.

(*Helps to Holiness*)

Introducing children to Jesus

I had a children's meeting one Saturday afternoon in Pennsylvania. Twenty-three children came and knelt at the penitent-form.

At one end there was a little boy. I knelt beside him and said, 'Darling, what do you want?'

He said, 'I want to get saved from my sins.'

'What are your sins?' I asked.

He replied, 'I quarrel with my little sister.'

We prayed together and he got saved.

Finally I came to the other end of the penitent-form and found a little girl. 'Darling, what do you want?'

'I want to get saved from my sins. I quarrel with my

brother.' She was at one end and he was at the other! I prayed with her too, and she trusted Jesus.

When they got up, they told each other they were sorry. Both are now Salvation Army officers. Years later, when I was lying in hospital, a young officer came to give me his blood in a transfusion. When I looked across the table to see who it was, it was that little boy.

(Adapted from *Portrait of a Prophet* by Clarence Hall)

We are not saved by doctrines

If you are trying to help a person know God, do not tell them they must believe this or that truth, as if faith is nothing more than believing certain things.

God does not hand us a volume of theology and say, 'Believe these truths and you will be saved.' He offers us his Son, and says, 'Believe in the Lord Jesus, and you will be saved' (Acts 16:31).

Truths are important, doctrines are valuable. Bad doctrine can send people floundering on the rocks of confusion and doubt. But don't try to argue a person into the Kingdom as if you must persuade them to agree with your beliefs. It is not an orderly system of truths, but 'the truth' that people need. It is not a book of doctrines, but a person, that God offers us. 'Yet to all who received him, to those who believed in his name, he gave the right to become children of God' (John 1:12).

It is not the acceptance of certain doctrines, but a penitent and childlike faith in a Saviour that saves. It is faith in him and loyalty to him that gives a person peace and purity and power.

The person who gives herself up to Christ will have a revelation of Christ in her own soul. God will unveil himself. She will come to know Jesus Christ.

Tell your friends to trust in Jesus Christ.

(*Resurrection Life and Power*)

A man in Christ

'I knew a man in Christ,' wrote Paul (2 Corinthians 12:2). That's a strange expression. Nobody would ever write: 'I knew a man in Napoleon, in Buddha, in Lincoln.' It is a startling expression, and yet Paul frequently spoke about being 'in Christ.'

He meant the Christian person is united with Christ. The life of Christ is in a man. He does not merely believe in Christ; he is connected with Christ and Christ lives within him.

I knew a man in Christ whose children said, 'It is easy to be good when dad is around.' His Christlike presence brought it out of them.

I knew a man who had been a hard, brutal drunkard, but was now a blacksmith 'in Christ.' One day a farmer brought his mare to this blacksmith to have her shod. He brought along straps because the horse was so difficult nobody could get near her to put on shoes unless she was strapped. But the blacksmith 'in Christ' said, 'Let me get acquainted with her.' He walked around her, stroked her gently, and spoke to her kindly and softly, while she rubbed her nose against him, smelled his clothes.

She seemed to discover that this was a new creature—a kind she had never met before, especially in a blacksmith's shop. Everything about him seemed to say to her, 'Don't be afraid,' and she was not afraid. He lifted her foot and took off a shoe, and from that day onwards he shod that mare without strap or tackle, while she stood in perfect quiet. Poor horse, she had waited all her life to see one of the sons of God, and when she saw him she was not afraid.

(*Love Slaves*)

Who is the Holy Spirit? (Part 1)

The Holy Spirit is the key to living the Christian life. He is the breath that enlivens us to God, the wind which powers and directs us. Yet for some, the Holy Spirit remains a mystery. Who is the Holy Spirit?

1. The Holy Spirit is a divine person.

First of all, the Holy Spirit is a person. This is how the Bible speaks of him. For example, Luke tells us that while certain Christians in Antioch were worshipping and fasting, 'the Holy Spirit said, "Dedicate Barnabas and Saul for the special work to which I have called them." So after more fasting and prayer, the men laid their hands on them and sent them on their way' (13:2-4 *NLT*). Notice:

Barnabas and Saul were sent out by the Holy Spirit. The Holy Spirit 'said' and the Spirit 'sent'.

Later, Luke says: 'Next Paul and Silas travelled through the area of Phrygia and Galatia, because the Holy Spirit had prevented them from preaching the word in the province of Asia at that time. Then coming to the borders of Mysia, they headed north for the province of Bithynia, but again the Spirit of Jesus did not allow them to go there' (16:6,7 *NLT*). Notice: the Spirit prevented them, as a person might prevent you entering a room.

Earlier on, when Peter was in Joppa and messengers from Cornelius, the Roman centurion, were looking for him, 'the Spirit said to him, "Simon, three men are looking for you. So get up and go downstairs. Do not hesitate to go with them, for I have sent them"' (Acts 10:19, 20). The Spirit spoke to Peter.

These few sentences are typical of the Bible, the way it establishes the personality of the Holy Spirit. Do not think of the Holy Spirit as merely a force or a power; he wills and acts and speaks; he is a person. He is the third Person in the Trinity.

Therefore you can know him. You too can hear him speak and experience his leading—or preventing.

2. The Holy Spirit is a presence.

Second, the Holy Spirit is also a presence. A person who sits in a room with you is a presence in that room. You know he is present; you do not just believe he is there, you realise it in experience. He may do things to you, he may speak with you. It is the same with the Spirit of God. He is a presence.

Picture the scene: Peter is standing in front of the High Priest and the Council which had condemned Jesus to death. Without any apparent fear, he tells them: 'The God of our ancestors raised Jesus from the dead after you killed him by hanging him on a cross ... We are witnesses of these things and so is the Holy Spirit, who is given by God to those who obey him' (Acts 5:3-32 *NLT*). So the Holy Spirit was a witness to the resurrection of Christ. In other words, he was there and now he is convincing men and women that Jesus is alive.

The Spirit is not a theory, he is a presence.

(*When the Holy Ghost is Come*)

Who is the Holy Spirit? (Part 2)

The Bible teaches us first, that the Holy Spirit is a divine person, the third person in the trinity. Second, he is also the presence of God among us. How else may we understand the Holy Spirit?

3. The Holy Spirit is the Counsellor

Third, the Holy Spirit is a wonderful counsellor. In my travels I have met marvellous counsellors, men and women of God who could understand life's burdens and offer just the comfort needed. The Holy Spirit is like that, and more. He comforts, but he says, 'Go forward. Do not give up. Face life with God. I will help you.'

During his final supper, Jesus spoke to his disciples about his departure, and he told them: 'I will ask the

Father, and he will give you another Counsellor to be with you forever— the Spirit of truth. The world cannot accept him, because it neither sees him nor knows him. But you know him, for he lives with you and will be in you' (John 14:16,17). Notice, Jesus said he was going away, but another would come who would take his place. That's the Holy Spirit. He will not go away, but stay with you for ever, and he 'will be in you.'

The King James Version calls him our Comforter. John, writing in Greek, called him *paraclete*. The word means, 'one called in to help: an advocate, a helper.' The same word is used to describe Jesus in 1 John 2:1: 'We have an advocate with the Father, Jesus Christ the righteous' (*NRSV*). Jesus is our advocate in Heaven, while the Spirit is our advocate on earth. Just as Jesus helped and taught the disciples on earth, now the Spirit helps and teaches Jesus' disciples.

He is the counsellor.

4. The Holy Spirit is the Empowerer

Fourth, the Holy Spirit is the one who empowers the followers of Christ.

Before he left this earth, Jesus commissioned his disciples to 'go into all the earth' with the message of the

Gospel. He was sending them to a world which did not wish to hear that message. They were to attack ancient systems of evil and entrenched sin. How could they possibly succeed? Through the Holy Spirit.

Jesus explicitly taught them to rely on the Spirit's supernatural work. 'When he comes,' said Jesus, 'he will convict the world of guilt in regard to sin and righteousness and judgment' (John 16:8). The Spirit will bring conviction.

The followers of Christ were weak, but the Spirit would strengthen them deep inside. So Paul would later pray, 'that out of his glorious riches he may strengthen you with power through his Spirit in your inner being' (Ephesians 3:16).

The Holy Spirit could enable because he is the source of spiritual power. Jesus promised his disciples, 'You will receive power when the Holy Spirit comes on you; and you will be my witnesses in Jerusalem, and in all Judea and Samaria, and to the ends of the earth' (Acts 1:8).

5. The Holy Spirit is ever-present

Fifth, the Holy Spirit is ever-present. It must have been wonderful to be a disciple and walk the hills of Galilee with Jesus. It must have been so good to enjoy a meal with

Jesus, to hear him teach, to ask him questions face to face. But the disciples could not be with Jesus every minute.

Jesus could not be everywhere at once. Sometimes he was on the mountains, while the disciples were in the valley vainly trying to cast out stubborn devils. One time he was on the shore while they were rowing on the wind-tossed sea. Another day he was disputing with the teachers of the law, and the disciples had to wait till he was alone to ask him to explain his teaching.

The Holy Spirit is different. They were never going to lose this counsellor in the crowd. No crisis would ever separate them from him. They could travel anywhere—to India where Thomas travelled, to Rome as Peter did, and he would be with them.

This was not Jesus in front of them—wonderful as that was. This was the Spirit in them and with them.

The Holy Spirit and you

So then, who is the Holy Spirit?

He is the Third Person in the Trinity. He is the presence of God with us, the power of God in us, the ever-present counsellor for us.

He is all that for you, if you trust in Christ, admit

your sinfulness and need of forgiveness and new life, and receive the Holy Spirit into your life. He is there for you to know. Trust him. Ask him to make himself more and more real to you. Surrender your life to him and ask him to fill you. Look for him, notice him, listen to him, rely on him, obey him—the Holy Spirit. And worship him as God.

(*When the Holy Ghost is Come*)

Christian Holiness

A clean heart

God wants you to have a clean heart.

What is a clean heart? It is an undivided heart. It belongs to God alone, and does not try to serve both God and self, or God and this world. It is a changed heart, no longer at the mercy of pride and selfishness and anger and filth and jealousy.

How can we have a clean heart?

First, be sure your sins are forgiven. That means you need to confess them and take them to the Cross.

If you have wronged anybody, undo the wrong so far as you can. Zacchaeus the tax collector said to Jesus, 'Look, Lord! Here and now I give half of my possessions to the poor, and if I have cheated anybody out of anything, I will pay back four times the amount' (Luke 19:8).

Second, now that you are forgiven, come to him with your will, your affection, your very self. Ask him to cleanse you from every dark passion, from every selfish wish, from every secret doubt. Ask him to come and fill your heart and keep you pure. Give your life up for his glory.

Then struggle no more. Instead, walk in the light he gives you, and patiently, expectantly trust him to answer your prayer. And as sure as you live, you shall soon, 'be filled to the measure of all the fullness of God' (Ephesians 3: 19).

(*Helps to Holiness*)

Sanctification vs consecration

A state senator's wife attended a series of our holiness meetings, and apparently became quite interested. One day she came to me, and said, 'Mr Brengle, I wish you would call it "consecration" instead of "sanctification". We could all agree on that.'

'But I don't mean consecration, sister; I mean sanctification; and there is a big difference between the two,' I replied.

This woman's mistake is a very common one. She wanted to rob religion of its supernatural element and rest in her own works. She could consecrate herself to God—she had control over that. But it is God who must sanctify us—that is, make us Christ-like.

Of course, men and women must be consecrated—

that is, given up to God—in order to be sanctified. We must yield our inner self, our mind and will, our tongue, our hands, our reputation, our doubts and fears, our likes and dislikes, our disposition to talk back at God.

But when we have done that, we must wait for God. We pray to him with a humble, persistent faith, asking him to fill our lives and make us pure. He promised to do it, and he will do it.

(*Helps to Holiness*)

Breaking free

How can a person break free from those sins which bring him undone time and again? Where does the power to break free come from?

From Jesus. From the same Jesus that saved you. The same Jesus who died for you.

But what is our part? What do we do? We need to put faith into action. What will that mean? Here are three valuable things we may do.

1. We must believe in God so genuinely that we make a complete break with sin. That is, we hate it because it is against God; we confess and repent before God.

2. We must trust God so genuinely that we surrender our life to him.

3. We must trust Jesus like the lepers and blind men did, and ask him to help us.

Look at it this way. If you knew you had to die very soon, what would you do? You would give yourself to God. If you had any grudges against any person, you would give them up, and if you had the opportunity you would ask them to forgive you. You would not stop to think how they would treat you. You would not care.

If you had robbed any man, you would try to restore to him what was his. If you had any selfish plans or ambitions, they would sink into mole hills before the mighty mountains of eternity, and you would give them up quickly. If you had been unfaithful in the discharge of any duty, you would confess it, and do all in the limited time left you to make the matter right.

Then, you would throw up your hands in helplessness, and ask God to forgive you for Jesus' sake, and not because there was any merit in yourself. And if you really trusted, you would receive forgiveness, and be at peace.

Now you would be a candidate for breaking free.

Well hopefully you are not soon to die. But you could settle these things today. You could forgive your enemies, confess your sins, surrender all to God.

Why not do it? Then ask the Lord to make you clean. He will do it. This is just what he wants to do.

(*Heart Talks on Holiness*)

The temptations of the sanctified person

When the Holy Spirit fills our life, when we are totally surrendered to God, we discover that many of the old temptations no longer trouble us. God has cleaned away some of the rubbish of our unregenerate self.

If a person was proud; now he may be no longer. If he once used bad language, he feels no inclination to any more. He now enjoys the liberty of the sons of God—because 'it is for freedom that Christ has set us free' (Galatians 5:1).

But while Christ has set this person free, the person has a continual warfare with Satan to keep this liberty. This warfare is what Paul calls 'the good fight of faith' (1 Timothy 6:12). And so now the person may encounter a different kind of temptation.

Here is one example. Satan will accuse him of sin

when the man's conscience is clear. Satan knows if he can get the person to listen to this accusation, the person will become discouraged and turn to introspection.

Here is the difference we need to notice:

- The devil *accuses* us of sin.

- The Holy Spirit *convicts* us of sin.

If I tell a lie, get proud, or break any of God's commandments, the Holy Spirit will convict me at once. But even when I have not sinned, Satan will accuse me of having sinned. The Bible says Satan is 'the accuser of our brothers' (Revelation 12:10).

For instance, a godly man talks to a non-Christian, urges him to give his heart to God, but the person does not. Then Satan begins to accuse the Christian: 'You did not say the right things; if you had, he would have given in to God.' It is of no use arguing with the devil. The only thing the man can do is to look away from the accuser to the Saviour and say: 'Lord, you know that I did the best I could at the time, and if I did anything wrong or left anything unsaid, I trust in your forgiveness through Christ's Cross.'

That settles it.

(*Helps to Holiness*)

You don't need more power

Do not keep chasing more spiritual power. Instead, ask to become a channel for the power of the Holy Spirit who is now in you.

Believe God, and do not obstruct the way of the Holy Spirit, so that he may work through you. Ask him to teach you, that you may not prevent his work.

Try to think his thoughts, to speak his words, to feel his love, and exercise his faith. Ask him to help you pray when he wants you to pray, speak when he wants you to speak, and be silent when he wants you to be silent.

'Keep in step with the Spirit' (Galatians 5:25).

(*Helps to Holiness*)

The heart of Jesus

Jesus had a humble heart. He said: 'I am gentle and humble in heart' (Matthew 11:29). He, 'had equal status with God but didn't think so much of himself that he had to cling to the advantages of that status no matter what. Not at all. When the time came, he set aside the privileges of deity and took on the status of a slave, became human! Having become human, he stayed human. It was an incredibly humbling process. He didn't claim special privileges. Instead, he lived a selfless, obedient life and then died a selfless, obedient death—and the worst kind of death at that—a crucifixion' (Philippians 2:5-8 *TM*).

Though he was the Lord of life and glory, he stooped to be born in a manger, and worked as an unknown carpenter for 30 years. While Jesus never seemed ill at ease in the presence of those who had 'greatness' or learning, he found friends among the hardworking, ordinary people.

Just a short time before his death, he took the place of a slave, and washed his disciples' feet, and then said, 'I have set you an example that you should do as I have done for you.' (John 13:15).

That helped me so much in the training college. The second day I was there they sent me down into a dark little cellar to black half a cart-load of dirty boots for the cadets. The devil came at me, and reminded me that, a few years before, I had graduated from a university, that I had spent a couple of years in a leading theological school, had been pastor of a metropolitan church, had just left evangelistic work in which I saw hundreds seeking the Saviour, and that now I was only blacking boots for a lot of ignorant lads.

But I remembered the Lord, and the devil left me. That little cellar was changed into one of Heaven's ante-rooms, and my Lord visited me there.

If you are going to have a heart like Jesus, it will be humble. And that means a practical, everyday humility. 'Clothe yourselves with humility' (1 Peter 5:5).

(*Helps to Holiness*)

Tithing

I gave back to God ten percent of my money when I was getting my education and was so poor I ate oatmeal almost exclusively.

At that time I was living on borrowed money, and I gave my tenth from that. The devil said, 'Why do you do this? This is not your money, it belongs to your creditors.'

I said, 'You're a liar. This is my Father's money; its only passing through my hands, and he will have a tenth!'

And God looked after me, as his Word promises he will. In a remarkably short time I was able to pay back every cent I owed.

(Adapted from *Portrait of a Prophet* a biography by Clarence Hall)

Temptation

You will never be free from temptation. The holiest person is still tempted. Our Lord was tried and tempted for 40 days and 40 nights by the devil, and the servant must not be surprised if he is tempted also.

It is no sin to be tempted; in fact, the apostle James tells us to be glad when we are tempted because the resulting trial of our faith will produce in us strength and force of character (James 1:2-4). Just as storms twist the roots and toughen the fibres of an oak tree, temptation helps to form our moral character.

No doubt Moses was tempted by the luxury of Pharaoh's court, but 'he chose to be mistreated along with the people of God rather than to enjoy the pleasures of sin for a short time' (Hebrews 11:25). And Moses became the great law giver.

Daniel was tempted by the wine from Nebuchadnezzar's table, and remember he was far from home. But he 'resolved not to defile himself with the royal food and wine, and he asked the chief official for permission not to defile himself this way'(Daniel 1: 8). And Daniel went on to receive the highest honours the king could give.

These temptations proved to be turning-points in their lives. God taught and strengthened them until he could pile on their shoulders the cares and perplexities of a nation, and they would not fail him.

And we, in turn, and according to our strength and duties, must be tested.

(*Heart Talks on Holiness* and *Resurrection Life and Power*)

Promises for the tempted

When you find yourself about to do wrong, that is what the Bible calls temptation, or a test. When you think of taking matters into your own hands rather than doing things God's way, that too is a temptation. When you feel a powerful urge to vent your anger wrongly or to cheat or to shade the truth or to boast or to give in to some other sin, that too is a temptation. If you hear the whisper telling you to quit on God, to go easy on God's service, to walk more on the world's road, that too is temptation.

The Bible is teeming with encouragements to tempted people.

1. It is a normal Christian experience

Be assured: 'No temptation has seized you except what is common to man' (1 Corinthians 10:13). You are not the first to be tested this way. Others have gone before and triumphed. You are not alone.

2. God knows your limits

'God is faithful; he will not let you be tempted beyond what you can bear. When you are tempted, he will also provide a way out so that you can stand up under it' (1 Corinthians 10:13). God will not allow a trial to exceed our strength, if we will promptly look to him and seek his help. God allowed Satan to go only so far with Job (Job 1:12; 2:6), and he does the same with you.

3. Jesus understands—he was tempted too

Be encouraged by this great truth about Jesus: 'We don't have a priest who is out of touch with our reality. He's been through weakness and testing, experienced it all—all but the sin. So let's walk right up to him and get what he is so ready to give. Take the mercy, accept the help' (Hebrews 4:15,16 *TM*).

4. You can grow through this

Take the long view: 'Blessed is the man who perseveres under trial, because when he has stood the test, he will receive the crown of life that God has promised to those who love him' (James 1:12). How can the oak have strength and beauty unless it stands the storm? How can the soldier have the victory if he gives up the battle and runs away from the fight?

What, then, are we to do about temptation?

1. Avoid the danger if you can

Jesus told his disciples: 'Watch and pray so that you will not fall into temptation' (Matthew 26:41). Not every temptation is inevitable—if David had taken care and prayed, he would not have brought such criticism to the cause of God as he did with Bathsheba. Many tests can be avoided by carefulness and prayer.

2. Don't be discouraged

Don't be discouraged. James said, 'Consider it pure joy, my brothers, whenever you face trials of many kinds, because you know that the testing of your faith develops perseverance' (James. 1:2,3).

3. Ask God for strength and conviction

Look to God for victory. All Heaven is on our side. We may 'approach the throne of grace with confidence, so that we may receive mercy and find grace to help us in our time of need' (Hebrews 4:16).

(*Resurrection Life and Power*)

Intense temptations

Do not be surprised if you face intense temptations. Maybe you have just experienced a real breakthrough with God, or a time when he felt very real to you: don't be discouraged if you are then hit by fierce temptation.

Remember it was after Jesus was baptized that he was led into the wilderness to be tempted by the devil for 40 days and 40 nights (Matthew 4:1-7). 'A student is not above his teacher, nor a servant above his master,' Jesus said (Matthew 10:24). If he was tempted, you will be tempted too.

So don't be distressed by these temptations. 'Consider it a sheer gift, friends,' wrote James, 'when tests and challenges come at you from all sides. You know that under pressure, your faith-life is forced into the open and shows its true colours.' (James 1:2, 3 *TM*). Your trials and temptations will lead you into a deeper acquaintance with Jesus.

And Jesus truly understands. 'Since he himself has gone through suffering and testing, he is able to help us when we are being tested' (Hebrews 2:18 *NLT*). If you were going through an ordeal—at work or in your family or perhaps an illness—you would value a conversation with someone who has passed through a similar ordeal. You would expect they might understand. The Bible says about Jesus: 'This High Priest of ours understands our weaknesses, for he faced all of the same testings we do, yet he did not sin' (Hebrews 4:15 *NLT*).

(*Helps to Holiness*)

Christian conversation

Do not imagine blasphemy and bad language are the only forms of sinful talk. Many Christians who never swear, sin by other forms of wrong talk. Crowds of people have backslidden; many almost-Christians have turned back into darkness; and churches have become spiritual graves, all because of such sinful talk.

1. What are some examples of sinful talk?

• It is sinful to tell *lies* about any person, or *slander* him in any way. 'No lies about your neighbour!' God says (Exodus 20:16 *TM*). A man's reputation and character are sacred in the sight of God, and just as God forbids one man to rob another of his property, so he forbids him to rob him of his good name. Paul gave hard warning to the sexually immoral, to the greedy, the idol worshipper and the adulterer. But in the very same sentence he included slanderers (1 Corinthians 6:10)! 'Believers . . . must not slander anyone' (Titus 3:2 *NLT*). This is a command of God, and should be thought about and obeyed.

- It is wrong to *go on about the faults and weaknesses of others*. This is a very common form of sinful talk. It is beautiful the way children never appear to notice the disabled playmate's difficulty, and it is Christ-like when grown-ups overlook the faults and weaknesses in others.

- It is sinful to *tell others about any person's sins and wrongdoing where and when it will do no good*.

2. Who does sinful talk hurt?

Who do we wrong by sinful talk?

- First of all, *we wrong the person we are talking about*. You do not like any one to speak critically or pass on negative gossip about you. You consider it wrong for anyone to do so. But why? When you have answered you have given yourself a reason why you should not speak evil of any man.

- Second, *we wrong the one we are speaking to*. We fill their mind with unjust prejudice. Our talk excludes good thoughts, and it tempts them to think and speak wrongly.

- *Third, we harm ourselves.* We destroy generous and kind thoughts, and stifle love. We open our hearts for the devil to enter. Talk like that prevents us from praying in faith and love for the person, which would be infinitely better than speaking harmfully about him.

- Fourth, *we grieve the Holy Spirit* and break the commandment of God. The Holy Spirit leads us to love all men—even our enemies. He leads us to love them, just as Jesus loved them. But sinful-speaking destroys love. The Holy Spirit leads us to pray for all men, especially for those who are faulty and sinful. Sinful talk stifles the spirit of prayer as sure as water puts out a fire.

- Fifth, *we wrong Jesus.* He died for that person you speak about. He bought him with his blood. And even though the man may be a sinner, or a hypocrite, Jesus loves him. Jesus identifies with people so much, that he will say at the judgment, 'When you (gave food or water or shelter) to the least of these brothers and sisters, you were doing it to me' (Matthew 25:40 *NLT*). Unless we repent of sinful talk, at the judgment he will face us with the wrong as if it were done to himself.

(*Heart Talks on Holiness*)

The remedy for sinful talk

What is the remedy for sinful talk?

- *Put yourself in the other person's shoes.* Consider that he may have struggles you know nothing about. He may have business troubles and cares, or he may have family trials to which you are a stranger, or he may have had very faulty early training which has marred him for life. We ought to leave judgment to God, who knows all and is infinitely wiser and more merciful than we are.

- *Think about your own sins and faults.* This will be far more profitable than thinking about his. It is infinitely more likely to make a better person of you.

- *Remember the danger sinful talk poses to yourself.* One of the chief dangers in wrong-speaking is that we eventually under-estimate everybody else, and over-estimate ourselves. We see our own virtues and other people's faults, when we ought to look long at their virtues and at our own faults. If we want to be like Jesus, we must obey the command, 'In humility consider others better than yourselves' (Philippians 2:3).

- *Consider how Jesus loves the person.* If Jesus loved him enough to die for him, can't we love him too? And if the person is Christian, then he or she is a child of God. Your Heavenly Father is her Heavenly Father. Consider how a parent with four children loves them all, and is hurt when one of them is wronged. How much more does God love that person as well as you, and is hurt when she is wronged.

- *Get a clean heart, full of the Holy Spirit,* full of love, and then you will not have to criticise any man.

(*Heart Talks on Holiness*)

Spiritual power

If you are serving God, I imagine you would like to serve in the power of the Holy Spirit. The difference between plain human work and service in the power of the Spirit is like the difference between a light bulb on a shelf and a bulb connected and turned on.

God is the source of all spiritual power. How do we seek his powerful influence in our lives? There are two practical ways—by meditation on his Word, and by private prayer.

Several years ago I was guest preacher at a New England corps which was being led by a rather gifted officer. He appeared to be impressed by my familiarity with and use of the Bible. One day he said, 'I would give a fortune for an equal knowledge of the Scriptures.'

He was taken back when I assured him that he was quite mistaken as to the strength of his desire: if he really wanted to know his Bible, he would use the hour he gave each day to the newspapers.

People everywhere are wanting to be filled with the Spirit, but they neglect the means by which this fullness is secured. That is prayer and the word of God. Believing, private prayer, and patient, constant meditation in the word of God will keep the sanctified man full of power, full of love and faith, full of God. But neglect of these results in spiritual weakness. It leads to dryness, joyless work and fruitless effort.

The devil will rob us of this time if we do not fight for it. He will say, 'Go and work,' before we have gained the spiritual food that strengthens us for work. The Spirit will call you to prayer, all your best common sense will urge you to spend time with the Bible, but the devil will tell you the work is too important to be left another minute. The devil's piety and eager interest in God's work is amazing when he sees a man upon his knees!

Spend time alone with God, and you will see his influence growing in your life.

(*Heart Talks on Holiness*)

The radicalism of holiness

Friend, don't think you can make holiness popular. It cannot be done.

There is no such thing as holiness except 'Christ in you,' and it is an impossibility to make Christ Jesus popular in this world. To sinners and un-spiritual professing-believers, the real Christ Jesus has always been and always will be 'despised and rejected by men' (Isaiah 53:3).

The 'Christ in you' is 'the same yesterday, today, and for ever'—hated, reviled, crucified.

Do not waste your time trying to fix up a popular holiness. Just be holy because the Lord God is holy.

(*Helps to Holiness*)

Don't confess other people's sins

When you talk about sins, make sure they are your own and not other people's.

The habit of confessing other people's sins began right at the start of our troubles. 'Did you eat any fruit from that tree in the middle of the garden?' God asked Adam.

'It was the woman you put here with me,' the man said. 'She gave me some of the fruit, and I ate it' (Genesis 3:11,12 *CEV*). He blamed Eve. Then she blamed the snake. 'The snake tricked me,' she said (13).

Both of them confessed the other's sins instead of owning up to responsibility themselves. This, sadly, is the way with fallen humanity. Nothing is more typical of our natural spiritual deadness than this inability to face our own sins. It is so much easier to hide behind other people's faults.

'Are you saved?' I asked a little woman in one of our meetings.

'No, I am not,' she replied emphatically.

'Were you ever saved?' I asked.

'Yes, I was.'

'And what did Jesus do that you turned your back on him?' I asked.

'A man who called himself a Christian slapped my husband across the face,' she said; but she did not tell me the fact (which I learned later) that the man later apologized.

'Well, that was too bad,' I replied. 'But you know, they slapped Jesus in the face.' She looked at me. 'And you know they spat in his face also, and not content with that, they crushed a crown of thorns on his head; but that did not satisfy them, so they bared his back, and tied his hands and whipped him. They mocked him and crucified him.'

I continued: 'When he was dying there on the Cross he prayed, "Father forgive them." He did all that for you, but you turned your back on him because of someone who ill-treated your husband.'

Tears filled her eyes and she rushed, sobbing, to the penitent-form. And there she didn't confess the fellow's sins, but her own.

Friend, let me urge you take your eyes off other people and fix them on Jesus. Then make a habit of confessing your own sins. Remember what John wrote in his letter: 'If we claim that we're free of sin, we're only fooling ourselves. A claim like that is errant nonsense. On the other hand, if we admit our sins—make a clean breast of them—he won't let us down; he'll be true to himself. He'll forgive our sins and purge us of all wrongdoing (1 John 1:8,9 *TM*).

(*Love Slaves*)

Discipline your talk

People often fall into gossip and criticism, not so much from ill-will as from old habit. Or they drift along with the current of conversation. Or they want to say something entertaining so as to fit in. If we want to break the habit and avoid these traps, what should we do?

It is wise to replace the old habits with new habits. Make it your practice to think and speak true, positive, uplifting things. When a man seeks to rid his mind of wrong thoughts, he is wise to follow Paul's advice to the Philippians: 'Fix your thoughts on what is true, and honourable, and right, and pure, and lovely, and admirable. Think about things that are excellent and worthy of praise' (Philippians 4:8 *NLT*).

So practice speaking positively. Try praising others, look for their good qualities. Next time you are in a conversation that turns negative, deliberately insert kind words. You will be amazed at the result.

(*When the Holy Ghost is Come*)

Christian life

Do you have to be fed
with a spoon?

We were sitting together after the meeting. 'I was at the penitent-form,' he told me.

'Were you? I couldn't see you during the prayer time and wondered where you were.'

I had seen him sitting in the audience while the commissioner preached; he had a look on his face that puzzled me. I was not sure whether it was defiance, cynicism, questioning or indifference. When the prayer time began, every head was bowed, but he sat erect. People were melting and flowing down to the penitent-form, but still he sat there, eyes open, apparently unmoved. I knelt to deal with seekers, and when I looked again he was gone, and not till after the meeting did I learn that he had been to the penitent-form.

'Yes, I was at the penitent-form. An old officer came and asked if he could help me, but I told him, "No, I want to be left alone." I was angry.'

'Angry! What were you angry about?'

'Well, while I listened to the commissioner, I wondered, "Why don't our leaders feed us young ones? They don't have meetings with us. Why don't they help us?"'

I had up to that time thought of him as a youngster. He belonged to the younger set of officers. I had known him since he was a small lad, and I had always thought of him as a young man, but when he called himself a 'young fellow' my mind turned a somersault. I looked at him and asked, 'How old are you?'

'Thirty-five.'

'And you have been married 13 years and have a family of children, the oldest of whom is 12. You are not a young fellow. You are a middle-aged man. And you want your leaders to feed you. But that is not what you need. You need to feed yourself.'

'You don't pray enough. You do not search the Scriptures and feed on the Word of God as you should. "Man shall not live by bread alone, but by every word that comes from the mouth of God." Isn't that your trouble?

Do you deny yourself as you should? Do you search for soul-food in good books? Or do you not spend more time reading the sports page?'

What about you, my friend? Can you feed your own soul, or must you still be fed? Do you prepare your own soul-food, or do others prepare it for you?

'I will guarantee,' one young divisional commander told me, 'that I can send the most backslidden officer to the corps at W, and in three months the soldiers will have loved him and prayed for him and helped him catch fire with God.' Those soldiers were no longer spiritual babies. If their officers did not feed them, then they fed the officers. If nobody blessed them, they blessed somebody else.

One day Paul came to Corinth and 'he met a Jew named Aquila, a native of Pontus, who had recently come from Italy with his wife Priscilla . . . and because he was a tentmaker as they were, he stayed and worked with them' (Acts 18:1-3). But they later moved to Ephesus, and then one day a gifted preacher named Apollos came to the city, teaching about God. He was a great orator, but this tent-maker and his wife had learned more from Paul than Apollos knew. So they invited him home to dinner with them, 'and explained to him the way of God more adequately' (Acts 18:26). Aquila and Priscilla had learned to feed themselves.

I knew an officer who, when I first met him, was sodden with drink. But within a few days he was saved. Shortly after, he became an officer, and then got himself a small, but choice library of the most deeply spiritual books. He would sit up till after midnight reading, praying, and meditating on what he read, until in a short time I marvelled at him. His mind was alert, his soul was on fire and his mental and spiritual equipment was amazing. He worked for spiritual food, and he grew. And he was soon able to feed others. Whenever I met him he wanted to talk about spiritual things. His grasp of doctrine, his knowledge of Scripture, and his intimate acquaintance with God delighted and refreshed me.

Yes, officers should feed their soldiers; commissioners and divisional commanders should feed their officers. 'Take care of my sheep,' Jesus told Peter, and officers have the same responsibility. But both officers and soldiers should also learn to find spiritual food and to feed themselves.

(*Ancient Prophets*)

Jesus was not a whisperer

Jesus was not a whisperer. No one ever saw him close to his friend's ear, looking stealthily around in case someone should overhear what he was going to say. He stood up, looked men in the eye, and spoke frankly.

When he did speak privately to his disciples, he told them to shout it from the housetops. 'Truth fears nothing but concealment,' said an old Church Father, and Jesus spoke only the truth. 'For this reason I was born, and for this I came into the world, to testify to the truth' (John 18:37).

There was nothing dark and hidden about Jesus. He was and is the Light of the world, and he welcomed the light. He entered into no secret clubs and councils. He belonged to no clique or party faction. I really do not believe he would have joined a secret society, for two reasons. First, because if there was anything wrong and dark about it, he would have revolted against it. Second, if there was anything good in it, his generous spirit would never have been content til he could share it with everyone.

And now he wants us to 'follow in his steps' (1 Peter 1:21). If we do this we shall not be passing on rumours, we shall not listen to, or pass on gossip, or be whisperers.

People who speak in secret what they are afraid to speak openly, wrong their own souls and weaken their own character, while those who listen are filled with suspicions and dislikes. Gossip, criticism, slander all quench the spirit of prayer, and faith in God. Faith can flourish only in an atmosphere of frankness, kindness and good will.

Don't let yourself be a whisperer.

(*Ancient Prophets*)

Don't argue

Some years ago, in Boston, I attended an all-night of prayer. Right at the end, the pioneer Salvationist, Commissioner James Dowdle, spoke to people who had been to the penitent-form: 'Remember,' he urged them, 'if you want to retain a clean heart, don't argue!'

There were 20 years of practical holiness behind that advice, and it fell on my ears like the voice of God. A man or woman of God ought not be arguing with others.

The enemies of Jesus were constantly trying to tangle him in his words and questions, but he never argued. They came to him one day and asked whether it was right to pay taxes to Caesar (Matthew 22:21). Jesus asked for a coin, then asked them whose image was on the coin.

'Caesar's,' they replied.

'Give to Caesar what is Caesar's and to God what is God's,' said Jesus.

They got no argument from him.

It is normal for the natural mind to resent opposition, but we are to be 'spiritually-minded.' By nature we are proud of our opinions. We resist the person who sets himself against us. We defend what we believe in. We don't like being contradicted. We are hasty in judging other people's motives. We speak against those who hold different views to ourselves. There are all sorts of reasons why we argue. I am strongly inclined to believe that this is one of the last fruits of the natural mind which grace ever subdues.

But let us who share in the divine nature (2 Peter 1:4) see to it that this piece of our old nature is cast off and replaced by the nature of Christ.

(*Helps to Holiness*)

Let the one book
shape your life

If you want the truth to shape your life, you must read and re-read the Bible. Just as the student constantly refreshes his mind by reviewing his textbooks, you must constantly refresh your mind with the Scripture's truths. The truth will slip, if you do not refresh your mind.

The Bible is God's recipe book for making holy people. You must follow the recipe exactly, if you want to be a holy, Christ-like person.

The Bible is God's guide-book to show men and women the way to Heaven. You must pay strict attention to its directions, and follow them accurately, if you are ever to get there.

The Bible is God's medical book, to show people how to get rid of soul-sickness. You must diligently consider its diagnosis of soul-diseases, and its methods of cure, if you want soul-health.

Jesus said, 'Man does not live on bread alone, but on every word that comes from the mouth of God' (Matthew 4:4). He also said, 'The words I have spoken to you are spirit and they are life' (John 6:63).

Read God's Word.

(*Helps to Holiness*)

Make good use of time

The difference between wise men and fools, saints and sinners, does not usually result so much from the start they had in life as the difference in their use of time.

One redeemed it; the other squandered it. One was a miser of the minutes; the other was a big spender of days. The one was ever up and doing, packing into every hour some search for truth, some prayer to God, some service to man; the other was forever neglecting the opportunity of the present, but full of dreams for some future.

Never go on to the street or take a journey without at least a New Testament with you, and some other useful book if possible. And don't forget to use them. The Gospel of St. Matthew can be read through in two hours.

This may not be the most profitable way to read it, and yet it will pay to read it right through at one sitting, that we may see the life of Jesus as a whole as we would the life of any man. Paul's first letter to Timothy can be read in 20 minutes, while Jude can be read in three minutes easily. Don't throw away those minutes.

(*The Soul-Winners Secret*)

God does not make pets of his people

I don't suppose I have had an easy life.

I do not remember my father. He made the soldier's supreme sacrifice during the Civil War when I was a very little child, and my earliest recollections are of a bereaved and weeping mother.

In my adolescence I was away from home at school when I received my first telegram. It read: 'Come home. Come quickly. Mother is dying.' When I reached home my mother, who had taught me to pray, lay with folded hands, dead. For the next 12 years I had no home.

At the beginning of my Salvation Army career, a Boston rough hurled a brick at my head and laid me out for 18 months, and gave me a shock from which I have not completely recovered in 35 years.

In the midst of my Army career I was overseas when I was stricken down with an agonizingly painful and dangerous illness. I lay at death's door among strangers for weeks. Some years later, lying helpless in a hospital with a great surgical wound that threatened my life, word was brought to me that my wife, the darling of my heart, was dying.

And now at 64, I find myself battered and broken in an automobile accident.

Meaning

What do we make of the difficulties of life? I do not argue that these are the best things that could have happened to me. But I do testify that by God's grace, they have been made to work together for my good.

They have humbled me. They have thrown me back on God. They have made me think. They have led me to search the Bible and history to find out God's ways with man. They have been rigorous and unsparing teachers. From them I have learnt endurance, patience, sympathy and understanding.

They have taught me the solidarity of humanity, and gave my heart more sympathy and understanding with others. The truth is, danger, loss and suffering draw people together and make them realise they are all bound in one bundle of life. On the other hand, pleasures and plenty separate people into rival groups, contending for mastery and selfish interests, indifferent to the welfare of others.

Following the automobile accident, messages came in from near and far. Many asked questions such as: 'Why did this happen?' 'Why did it happen to you whose hands were so full of helpful work? Why not someone doing nothing?' 'Was it devil, man, or God that put you through this?'

Such questions are natural, but are they wise? Can we find any cut-and-dried answer? I don't believe we can.

Let me make this clear. We should not expect God will shield us from every trouble. God does not make pets of his people. He does not cotton wool those whom he draws into close fellowship. His greatest servants have often been the greatest sufferers. Out of their deep sorrow they have comforted others.

God has no interest in developing a race of molly-coddles. He could work miracles every day, saving children from bumping their toes and from tumbling down stairs, from burns when they disobey their parents and touch fire, from being crushed when they run in front of cars, from getting stomach-ache when they eat green apples, or from poverty when their father gambles or their mother runs off with another man. God could save them every time. But God does not work such miracles. And since he does not do it for children, we should not expect him to do it for adults.

We would be hopelessly spoiled if God did constantly rescue us. A human being must learn to think before he leaps; he must watch out for danger, just as a wild animal is alert for danger; he needs to develop courage in the face of opposition. A person must learn self-restraint, patience, sympathy, faith, a sense of his limitations. How would we develop any of these without difficulties and danger and hurts?

So no, God does not make pets of his people. But he does stay close with them, helping, comforting and strengthening them. He does work for good through the worst of tragedies and the hardest of disappointments. God is not defeated by troubles, and neither need his people be.

(*Resurrection Life and Power*)

Keep within
whispering distance of God

When an old seminary friend was leaving for his first church, I followed him on to the train to say good-bye. He looked up and said: 'Sam, give me a text that will do for a life motto.' Instantly I asked God for light.

Now that is one of the things you must constantly do—lift your heart to God and look to him for light, not only in the crises and great events of life, but in all its little and seemingly trifling details.

You can get into such a habit of doing this that it will become as natural for you as breathing, and it will prove quite as important to your spiritual life as breathing is to your natural life. Keep within whispering distance of God always.

Well, I proved to be in whisper touch with Jesus that morning on the train, and immediately the first eleven verses of the first chapter of 2 Peter were suggested to my mind.

(*Helps to Holiness*)

Speaking in tongues

The gift of tongues is hardly mentioned in the book of Acts, but in the church at Corinth it seems to have been a big thing. Paul had to help the Corinthians, and what he told them can help us also.

The Christians at Corinth were not healthy. They argued (1 Corinthians 1:11), they split over leadership (1:12; 3:1-7). They took each other to court (6:1-8); they held unsound views of marriage (chapter 7). Some were gluttons and others drunks (11:21); while others were conceited and spiritually proud (14:36, 37). It was not a healthy church.

The Apostle Paul wrote them a letter full of down to earth, spiritual instruction. In chapter 12 he mentions nine gifts of the Spirit. Tongues is listed at number eight, just one of the list. Yet the Corinthians attached so much importance to tongues that Paul devoted one of the longest chapters to the matter. From chapter 14 we learn:

1. When a person speaks in tongues, he is speaking with God, not to other people. Paul said, 'Anyone who speaks in a tongue does not speak to men but to God' (2). Therefore he should not speak in church, but keep silent, unless he or someone else interprets. 'If there is no interpreter, the speaker should keep quiet in the church and speak to himself and God' (28). 2. While speaking in an unknown tongue may build up the one who speaks, it does not build up those who hear. Paul wrote: 'The one who prays using a private "prayer language" certainly gets a lot out of it, but proclaiming God's truth to the church in its common language brings the whole church into growth and strength' (4 *TM*).

3. Instead of making sounds in church which are unintelligible, we should want to sing, pray and speak with understanding. He said, 'In a church meeting I would rather speak five understandable words to help others than ten thousand words in an unknown language' (19 *NLT*). The apostle is here, as always, intensely practical. He puts higher value on the useful than the spectacular.

4. Paul was not at all impatient with Christians who did speak in tongues. He respected the gift. 'Don't forbid speaking in tongues' he wrote (39 *NLT*)—once he has made clear that they should not speak in public unless there is an interpreter.

In the end, it was not tongues which Paul prized most, but love. Love would heal their divisions. Love would help those with the gift realise they are not spiritually more advanced than those without it.

Love will make people who do not speak in tongues respect those who do. And love will make those who speak in tongues exercise their gifts in private before the Lord.

(*Resurrection Life and Power*)

The prophets of the Bible

How do we read the prophets of the Bible? Are books such as Daniel, Jeremiah and Ezekiel to be read chiefly to find what they tell about the future?

Many think the prophets have put into our hands a God-given telescope through which we can peer into the future. But I have never been helped, but rather confused, by attempts to interpret the prophets in that way.

Their value to me has appeared to consist not in the light they throw upon generations yet unborn, but the light they throw upon my own generation. I want help to interpret my own times.

The prophets originally spoke to their own times, announcing God's message to the people. And in our times, their prophecies help me to understand the present, to recognize my own duty, to interpret the will and ways of God to the men of my own generation. Beyond that, if I see at all, it is but dimly.

Yes, there is an element of foretelling in the messages of the prophets, but the infinitely greater element was that of forth-telling. By that I mean telling about God himself, his character, his love. And it is in the light of this revelation of God's character and ways, that I can 'read' my own times and see my duty.

And this view of the supreme value of the prophets for our day seems to me to harmonize with Paul's statement of the great purpose of Scripture: 'All Scripture is God-breathed and is useful' not for predicting the future, but 'for teaching, rebuking, correcting and training in righteousness' (1 Timothy 3:16).

(*Ancient Prophets*)

Guidance

Every mature Christian who has asked for God's guidance will tell you God truly does lead his people. This is not at all an unusual experience.

But we must be wise in this matter. We need to understand how God guides us, and not take every event as a sign from God. How then does the Holy Spirit guide us?

1. Through the Bible.

God speaks through his Word, especially by revealing to us the character and spirit of Jesus and his apostles, and leading us to follow in their footsteps.

2. Through circumstances.

God speaks through the ordinary circumstances of our daily life.

3. Through other people.

God may speak through the wise counsel of godly and experienced people.

4. Through inner conviction.

Sometimes God gives us an inner conviction. As we pray, the conviction only increases. It is by this sovereign conviction that men are called to preach, to go to foreign fields as missionaries.

~

If we look for God's guidance in these reliable places, we will find it. Why then do people sometimes ask for guidance and not receive it?

1. Because they do not study God's Word.

They neglect the cultivation of their minds and hearts in the school of Christ. Read the Word, use spare moments to soak up God's Word, and you will be shaped by that Word.

2. Because they do not humbly accept circumstances as something God can use.

They do not think of them as part of the providences of God. They do not realise these events may be God's school in which he is training them for greater things. They wish to escape what God may not want them to run from.

3. Because they are not teachable.

Any person who is not humble and teachable is not going to be led by God.

4. Because they do not listen and obey.

They are self-willed; they want their own way. Someone has said, 'Very often people are really not asking God for his will, but for approval of their own will.' Paul took his orders from God. He said of himself, 'I was not disobedient to the vision from heaven' (Acts 26:19). He obeyed God at all costs, and so the Holy Spirit could guide him.

5. Because of fear and unbelief.

It was this fearfulness and unbelief that caused the Israelites to turn back and not go into Canaan, when Caleb and Joshua assured them that God would help them to possess the land. They lost sight of God and feared the giants and walled cities, and so missed God's way for them and perished in the wilderness.

6. Because of impatience and rush.

Some of God's plans for us unfold slowly; and we must patiently and calmly wait for him. It is never God's will that we should get into a hurry. He wants us to stand still when the pillar of cloud and fire does not move, and then pull up our tent when it does move (see Exodus).

(*When the Holy Ghost is Come*)

The dangers of middle age

I will never forget the shock and chill that went through the hearts of American Christians some years ago when an evangelist—with silver hair, the author of a number of books of great spiritual insight, and a mighty preacher—fell into sin. We read and hear much about the dangers of youth, but how little we hear about the dangers of the mid-life!

I was vividly reminded of this only recently, when a man in his late 50s stopped me on the street and asked for help. He told me about his sins and temptations; he was entangled in a web of evil which was dragging him down. The middle-aged are not safe from sensual temptation.

Nor are they safe from general spiritual danger. They may lose the freshness of their early experience, their 'first love.' There is nothing in the world so wonderful as the constant renewal of spiritual youth in the midst of the losses and disappointments of middle life. And there is nothing so sad as the gradual loss of fervour, of simplicity, of heart devotion, of hope, of genuine love.

The Psalmist told his soul to bless the Lord so that his youth—his soul's youth—would be renewed like the eagles (Psalm 103:1-5). But many, instead, fall into decay. This loss may steal upon us like a creeping paralysis if we do not watch and pray.

1. It may come through experience of the weakness and fickleness of man.

We are continually tempted to lean on men rather than on God and his Word. If we do that, and men fail, we feel as though the foundations are swept away. At such times the Tempter will whisper: 'What is the use of you trying to live a holy life?' Unless we immediately go to Jesus, and lift our eyes to God, a chill of discouragement and doubt will sweep over us. If we are careless, we may become cynical people.

There was nothing that filled me with greater admiration for William Booth than his freshness, his perennial youth, his unfailing faith in God and man—in spite of all the failures and backslidings which wounded him to the heart.

2. It may come through cares and responsibilities.

Moses was thronged with care, but he walked with God. Added to his whippings, imprisonments and shipwrecks, Paul had pressing upon him 'the care of all the churches' (2 Corinthians 11:28), but he prayed and gave thanks.

A distinguished writer has said, 'Comradeship with God is the secret. When Christ says, "Come to me, all you who are weary and burdened, and I will give you rest. Take my yoke upon you and learn from me," he does not invite us to lay aside our work; he offers us rest in our work. The promise is that he will teach such how to labour and how to bear their burdens so as not to be wearied by them.' This the lesson we need to put into practice at mid-life.

(*Love Slaves*)

Don't disobey the vision from heaven

D o you want your life to matter? Do you want to be able to look back one day and see how God has grown fruit through your life? Here you can learn from the apostle Paul. Few people have ever lived lives as fruitful as Paul's. What was his secret?

He said, 'I was not disobedient to the vision from heaven' (Acts 26:19).

Back in the days when Saul was harassing and pursuing the little flock of first Christians, Jesus met him near Damascus. Jesus met him just as surely as he meets men and women to-day. Many years later, when Paul, as he was called now, appeared before King Agrippa, he told him the story:

About noon, Your Majesty, as I was on the road, a light from heaven brighter than the sun shone down on me and my companions. We all fell down, and I heard a voice saying to me in Aramaic, 'Saul, Saul, why are you persecuting me? It is useless for you to fight against my will.'

'Who are you, lord?' I asked.

And the Lord replied, 'I am Jesus, the one you are persecuting. Now get to your feet! For I have appeared to you to appoint you as my servant and witness. You are to tell the world what you have seen and what I will show you in the future. And I will rescue you from both your own people and the Gentiles. Yes, I am sending you to the Gentiles to open their eyes, so they may turn from darkness to light and from the power of Satan to God. Then they will receive forgiveness for their sins and be given a place among God's people, who are set apart by faith in me.

And so, King Agrippa, I obeyed that vision from heaven (Acts 26:13-20 *NLT*).

For Paul, obedience meant social ostracism, banishment from home and friends, the overturning of all his plans and ambitions, a life of hardship and frequent opposition. Paul had to take on the immensely challenging task of taking the Gospel to cities as far away as Greece and Turkey. But the fruit of Paul's dedication was tremendous. God used him to grow churches and take his name even to Rome. Still today, around the world, millions read Paul's letters every day.

Listen and obey

It is so important that we, like Paul, obey the vision from heaven. If God speaks to us through his Holy Spirit, it is vital we listen and obey. When you have the sense there is something you ought to do, do it. When you feel a call to live a certain life for God, to fulfil a destiny, to give yourself to some great task—you must do it.

The reason some people's lives are not as fruitful as they could be is they disobey the vision from heaven.

A millionaire heard the Gospel, and the heavenly vision came to him. He saw the Cross and the 'straight gate' and the 'narrow way,' just as Paul did. But like the rich young man who came to Jesus, this man went away, saying, 'If it wasn't for all the people watching, I'd have gone forward to pray.'

Sooner or later the heavenly vision comes to all men. It comes in the whispers of conscience, in the strivings of the Spirit, in the calls of duty, in the moments of regret for a bad past, in moments of tenderness, in the crises of life, in the pleas of God's people. It comes in sickness and losses. It comes when we suffer crushed hopes, disappointed plans and thwarted ambitions. It even comes with ominous awareness when we realise there is an eternal judgment to come.

In all these experiences of life, Jesus hides himself. God hid himself in the burning bush, which Moses saw on Mount Horeb. Moses went up to the bush and heard God speak. Another person may have ignored the bush, or quickly forgotten God's words. Not Moses. Moses listened and then obeyed. In the same way, we must pay attention when Christ speaks to us out of a burning bush of disappointment or rebuke or conviction.

And so with you, if you think God might be speaking, giving you a vision for service, however humble it might be, listen and obey.

(*Heart Talks on Holiness*)

Christian Service

The show girl

The girls of the troupe were pretty, with pencilled eyebrows and outlandish dresses, and they mixed loudly with the men of the party. It was a troupe of theatrical people who, with the exception of another man and myself, filled the sleeper carriage in which I was to cross New Mexico. There was nothing in common between us, so it seemed to me, but I found my heart going out to them.

When the porter began to make up the berth for the night, one of the older girls, waiting, sat on the arm of one of the seats of my berth. I removed my coat from the seat and asked her to sit down. At first she hesitated—possibly she felt the lack of common interest as much as I did—because she saw me in full uniform. For a few moments we sat opposite each other in silence. I wanted to speak to her but hardly knew how to begin.

At last, however, I made some common-place remark about the weird desert through which we were passing, and soon we were in conversation. I asked her about her work, and she told me of the long hours they spent in play and rehearsal—from 10 to 12 every day—a matinee in the afternoon, and play again from 7.30 to 11.30, never getting to bed before 1 am. And I noticed that beneath the camouflage of makeup and golden hair she looked tired and, I thought, a bit world-weary and disappointed. I asked her if she didn't miss home life, and she told me she had a good home in Chicago, but that she got restless after spending two or three weeks there.

Home

I told her that I understood, and that I was sure that this restlessness would grow, and that I knew of only one cure—the cure St Augustine wrote about: 'You have made us for yourself, and our heart is restless til it rests in you.' I told her that our souls were too great to be satisfied with anything less than God himself, and that he is our rightful home and friend.

I told her that when I was a little boy, because of the death of my father, it was not the four walls of the house that made my home, but my mother herself. She was my soul's home. But eventually she, too, died, and then my soul found its true home in God. I told her about Jesus, and his great love and sacrifice for us all, and she listened quietly and intently.

And then she stood up and gave me her hand in a warm clasp and, looking deep into my eyes, thanked me so sincerely that I felt her soul was looking direct at mine. And then she was gone.

In those moments I felt the presence of Jesus among us now, still seeking the lost. And then I realized, it seemed as never before, how he was the friend of lost people, how he loved them and longed for them. That night he gave me a fresh baptism of love for the lost, the straying souls who are trying to find satisfaction without him.

At 3 o'clock in the morning, in the stillness and darkness, that weary troupe of players slipped out of the train so silently that I did not hear them go, and I may never see them again. But my life was touched by the chance meeting with them. The quiet talk with the girl who is beginning to be disillusioned and to feel the emptiness of all things without Christ, left a blessing in my soul that will remain.

Our General, William Booth, has called us to go for souls. They are all about us. We may feel awkward speaking about Jesus—at first. We may be hesitant, shy, and uncertain just what to say and how to begin. But I find if I lift my heart to God in secret prayer, the way opens and I can talk with almost anyone.

(*Resurrection Life and Power*)

The person God uses

A while ago I was talking with a Christian businessman who expressed an important truth:

'People are asking God to use them, but sometimes he cannot. There are plenty of people who come to me and want work in my store, but I cannot use them; they are not fit for my work. When I need someone, I have to go and advertise, and sometimes spend days trying to find a person who will fit the position, and then I have to try him out to see whether he can do it well. It's similar with God. Some people he cannot really use—they are not surrendered to him; they are not humble and teachable.'

He is right. God looks for the right person. He does not ask, 'Does this woman possess great natural abilities? Is she educated?' He asks, 'Is her heart right toward me?

Is she holy? Does she love much? Is she willing to walk by faith, and not by sight? Does she only chase 'the honour that comes from God'? Will she give up when I correct her and try to prepare her for greater usefulness?'

When God finds such a person, he will use her.

(*Helps to Holiness*)

Self-discipline is essential

Many Christians are committed to the fight but are self-indulgent.

If they like a thing they must have it, however much it may make them unfit for service. There are people who know cake and candy injure them, but they like these things, and so they over-indulge themselves, at the risk of grieving the Spirit of God, and destroying their health, which is the capital God has given them to do his work.

There are people who ought to know that a big supper before a meeting makes one drowsy and heavy. Their role is to stand between God and the people. But they are hungry, they like food, and so they tickle their palate, spoil their meetings, disappoint the hungry souls of the people, and grieve the Holy Spirit.

People who indulge their bodies in food and drink also often indulge them in sleep. They eat late at night, and sleep heavily and lazily next morning, and usually need a cup of strong coffee to clear their heads. Getting up late, the work of the day crowds upon them, and they have almost no time to pray and read the Bible. Then the cares of the day press upon them, and their hearts get full of things other than the joy of the Lord. Jesus must wait till they have done everything else before he can catch their ear. So their day is spoiled.

(*Helps to Holiness*)

From little things
big things grow

You want God to use you. You want him to use your efforts, to bring souls into the Kingdom through your corps. Then you must be prepared to start small.

None of history's epoch-making revivals began in a large way. Paul usually began in a city by speaking regularly in a synagogue—just a small meeting-place of the Jews—until he was excluded. Then he moved to some home or room that was opened to him. John and Charles Wesley began in the same humble way, and so did William and Catherine Booth.

Renewal among God's people and awakenings among the unsaved never begin in a great way. They begin the same way oak trees begin. There is nothing startling and spectacular about the beginning of an oak tree. In darkness, in loneliness, an acorn gives up its life, and the oak, at first only a tiny root and a tiny stem of green, is born out of the death of the acorn. In a similar way revivals are born, souls are won, the Kingdom of God comes.

Someone dies—dies to self interest, to the praise of men, to ambition—and lives for Christ, lives to save others. And then—souls are born into the kingdom of God, Christians are renewed and want to tell about Jesus. 'Unless a grain of wheat falls into the earth and dies, it remains just a single grain,' said Jesus, 'but if it dies, it bears much fruit' (John 12:24).

One New York pastor held a funeral in the parsonage. I mean he died to his own interests. Day and night he cried to God for people to get saved. Every afternoon he was out visiting the people in their homes, their offices, their shops. For a month he devoted hours to the Bible, to reading the biographies of soul-winners, and books on revivals. He studied Calvary. He meditated on eternity. He stirred up his pity and compassion for the people. He repeatedly asked God to fill him with power, faith, and love. He enlisted members of his church who were spiritual to help him. When he won a person for Christ, he enlisted him as a helper in the fight. And God swept the church with revival fire, and hundreds were won to Christ.

This is the road Jesus himself took. Jesus, 'endured the cross, scorning its shame,' to save. He told his disciples, 'If anyone would come after me, he must deny himself and take up his cross and follow me' (Matthew 16:24). That is the way to become a soul-winner; that is the price that must be paid. The Master could find no easier way, and he can show no easier way to us. It is costly. But do we want to win eternal values cheaply?

Of course we can go on without offering our selves. We may work at the surface of people's lives, we may touch their emotions, we may lead them to religious activity. And we might think we are doing God's work. But we do not really win people until we follow Christ through death and into holiness.

Some years ago I went to a large city, where The Salvation Army owned a hall seating nearly a thousand people, and where I thought we had a flourishing corps. The officer and his wife had unusual ability, but had become stale and spiritually lifeless. Where hundreds should have greeted me, 50 tired, listless people were present.

Little had been organised. When I rose to give out the first song, there were three song-books among us, one of which was mine. The officer ran off downstairs to pick up a few more books, and while we waited I was fiercely tempted to walk off the platform and leave the place, telling him I would not spend my strength helping a man with so little interest.

Then I looked at the people in front of me—tired miners, struggling wives, and little, un-shepherded children—peering at me with quizzical eyes as if they wondered whether I would club them or feed them. They were 'sheep without a shepherd.' So I set myself to bless and feed them. And over the next six days the big hall was crowded and we were glad to see over 90 people seeking the Saviour. You see, we can begin with no advantages at all, but only our surrender to Christ, and then let him use us.

Be prepared to start small.

(*Ancient Prophets*)

Spiritual leadership

Spiritual leadership is not won by promotion, but by many prayers, confessions of sin and heart-searchings before God. It is not won by talent and hard work, but by self-surrender and a courageous sacrifice of every idol, and an uncompromising and uncomplaining embrace of the Cross.

It is not gained by seeking great things for our selves (Jeremiah 45:5), but rather, like Paul, by counting those things that were gain, loss for Christ. Hear him: 'But whatever was to my profit I now consider loss for the sake of Christ. What is more, I consider everything a loss compared to the surpassing greatness of knowing Christ Jesus my Lord, for whose sake I have lost all things. I consider them rubbish, that I may gain Christ' (Philippians 3:7,8).

That is a great price, but it must be unflinchingly paid by whoever would be not merely a nominal, but a real spiritual leader of others. Moses gained this spiritual leadership among Pharaoh's palace halls and Sinai's solitudes when he 'refused to be known as the son of Pharaoh's daughter. He chose to be mistreated along with the people of God rather than to enjoy the pleasures of sin for a short time' (Hebrews 11:24,25).

Spiritual leaders are not made by man, nor any combination of men; neither conferences, nor councils can make them, but only God.

Spiritual power is the outcome of spiritual life. Therefore let those who aspire to this leadership pay the price, and seek it from God.

(*The Soul-Winners Secret*)

The leakage
of spiritual power

I knew an officer once who let all his spiritual power leak out, and when he got into the meeting he was as dry as a bone.

It happened this way. We had to ride three miles in a street car to get to the hall, and all the way he was talking about things that had no bearing on the meeting. Nothing he said was wrong, but it was not to the point. It turned his mind from God and the people he was soon to face. The result was, that instead of going before the people clothed with power, he went stripped of power. I remember the meeting well. His prayer was good, but there was no power in it. It was just words! The Bible reading and talk were good. He said many true and excellent things, but there was no power in them. The Christians looked indifferent, the newcomers looked sleepy, and altogether the meeting was dull.

Now the officer was not losing his faith; he had a good experience. Nor was he without talent. The trouble was that, instead of keeping quiet and communing with God, he had wasted his power in useless talk.

Leakage

There are many ways to let power leak away.

I knew a soldier who came to the hall very early, and instead of getting his soul keyed up, spent the time playing soft, dreamy music on his violin. I have known men whose power leaked out through a joke. They believed in having the meeting go with a swing, and so they told funny stories and played the clown to make things lively. And things were lively, but it was not with divine life. It was the liveliness of humanity only, and not of the Holy Spirit. I do not mean by this that a man who is filled with the power of the Spirit will never make men laugh. He will; he may say tremendously funny things. But he will not be doing it just to have a good time. It will come naturally. It will not be dragged in on all fours, and it will be done in a consciousness of God, and not in a spirit of lightness and joking.

Any person who wants a meeting of life and power should remember there is no substitute for the Holy Spirit. He is life. He is power. And if he is sought in earnest, faithful prayer, he will come.

I know of a man who, if possible, gets alone with God for an hour before every meeting, and when he speaks it is with the power and demonstration of the Spirit. He is a model of the kind of approach to take. The Holy Spirit should be sought in earnest, secret prayer. Jesus said, 'When you pray, go into your room, close the door and pray to your Father, who is unseen. Then your Father, who sees what is done in secret, will reward you' (Matthew 6:6).

The person who wants power must walk with God. She must be a friend of God. She must keep the way always open between her heart and God. God will be the friend of such a person, and will bless her and honour her. God will tell her his secrets; he will show her how to reach hearts. God will be on her side and help her.

(*Helps to Holiness*)

Letter to a young officer

Get your time systematized. Don't let it fritter away. Hold yourself to a program as far as possible, and you will find yourself 'growing in favour with God and with man' (Luke 2:52). Plan your work early in the day and then work your plan.

Have a good long time alone with God each day, and have your colleague do the same. If you cannot take one long time, break it up. Take time to be holy, and give God time to talk to you, mould you, teach you.

Be sure and have the time of prayer and Bible study every day and your soul will become like a lush garden. This is the top priority. We have to work at our own hearts first, then work for others becomes easy and a joy.

Try this: when you wake up in the morning, do some

vigorous gymnastics, have a quick bath, and then go to your Bible and get on your knees. If that does not suit you, find another time, and pray briefly at the start of the day. But make a regular time! If you make this the habit of your life, you will grow.

And when you are with God, expect him to speak with you. Have a notebook with you to write down any thoughts and directions God gives you.

At least once a week, pray for each of your people, young and old, by name. Ask the Lord to show you their needs and how you can best help them. Carry them in your heart. Love them. They are the lambs and sheep of Jesus.

PS Read John's letter on your knees!

(From *Peace Like a River*, a biography by Sallie Chesham)

Preparing to preach

A young theologian asked me about my sermon preparation. This is what I told him: When I am preparing to preach, I don't only prepare the sermon, I prepare myself. I spend a great deal of time preparing myself to preach.

How? Prayer and Bible study are the chief factors.

Many make the mistake of giving more time to the preparation of their addresses than to the preparation of their own hearts, emotions and faith. The result is often fine, brilliant words that have the same effect as holding icicles in front of a freezing man. To warm others—isn't that your purpose in preaching?—a person must keep his own fire burning.

(From *Portrait of a Prophet* by Clarence Hall)

Counselling seekers

I want to give you some guidance on how to help people who come forward in meetings to kneel at the penitent form (or mercy seat). Here are some practical principles to help you when you are counselling seekers.

1. Give the person time alone with God. Permit me to suggest that, when people have reached the penitent-form they be allowed to kneel in silence before the Lord for a time without having people come to question them or pour advice into their ears. Give them an opportunity to listen to God's voice, and then let some wise soul go to them and say, 'Is there anything I can do to help you, or do you prefer to pray alone?'

2. *Always first lead the person to state clearly their own need.* Many come forward with only vague ideas, hardly knowing what they want and not having any idea how to find it. So help him think it through. If you allow him to explain his need, that will clarify it for him, it will bring the issue out of the fog to where it can be dealt with.

3. *Don't make salvation too easy.* Make it plain that before God can forgive sins, we must admit to our sins. If we can, we must be willing to make restitution for wrongs. We must be prepared to break with known wrongs. Ask them about that.

4. *Don't suggest the holy life comes cheaply.* There is a cost to being Jesus' disciple. Help them see they must put away all un-Christlike things, they must forgive their enemies, they must consecrate themselves entirely to God, and claim his promises.

5. *Speak with grace and tact, relying on the Holy Spirit*, so that the bruised reed is not broken, the smouldering flame is not put out (Matthew 12:20).

6. *Use your Bible.* Of all the words you speak as a counsellor, the words of Scripture should take up a large part. Learn where to find the promises of God in the Bible. Show the seeker these promises; help him read them for himself. Ask him to repeat it so it sinks in. And of course you have Bible stories you can call on. Tell them a story which shows how the Saviour dealt with people.

7. *Help them understand what they are doing, what they can expect to receive from God.*

8. *Avoid pressure or emotionalism.* Especially—do not bombard the seeker with too much advice.

9. *Do not hurry people.* Give God a chance to deal with them.

(From *Portrait of a Prophet* by Clarence Hall)

Letter to a troubled colleague

My dear friend, I read in your letter that you are, 'absolutely useless to God and man.' You are so tired and worn out, I am sure you are not seeing things as they truly are.

You say in your note to me: 'I was born to fight.' Now you are ill, you feel you are out of the fight, and you feel useless. But think about this: some of the busy activity you have been doing was no great spiritual fight. When you were at the head of a lot of shouting men and women the devil may have sat down and crossed his legs and watched it all as a performance. But he is on the job now. He is thinking, 'I will crush him.'

Don't imagine you are out of the fight. You are exhausted, sick, and needing rest, perhaps you are depressed, but you are not out of the fight. You are in it, and must now fight the fight of faith.

We in The Salvation Army put a lot of value in activity—not too much but too exclusively. We don't make enough of other parts of the Christian's life. The great battles, the battles that decide our destiny and the destiny of generations still unborn are not fought on public platforms, but in lonely hours of the night and in moments of agony.

Yes you were born to fight, but do not misunderstand the spiritual fight. 'Our struggle is not against flesh and blood' (Ephesians 6:12). It is not activity Paul called us to in this fight. He advised, 'Take the helmet of salvation and the sword of the Spirit, which is the word of God. And pray in the Spirit on all occasions with all kinds of prayers and requests. With this in mind, be alert and always keep on praying for all the saints' (Ephesians 6:17,18).

You can do that can't you, my friend? You can fight the fight of faith.

(From *Portrait of a Prophet* by Clarence Hall)

Take care of God's people

I was on a train once, when General William Booth spoke to a group of us. He said, 'Take care of the fire in your own souls, because the tendency of fire is to go out.'

It is true, isn't it. Spiritual fires may go out. I have been a travelling evangelist, and I can say the saddest thing is to see people begin with God, then lose the fire of the Holy Spirit within. Sometimes this is because nobody took the time to carefully nurture them. If you want to be a soul-winner, you must care for converts as well as save sinners. You must fan the new flame in their hearts and teach them how to care for it so that it never goes out. How?

1. They should be visited. Some time ago I called at a corps in California. The officer met me at the train, and on the way to the quarters remarked, 'We got one of the worst alcoholics in town saved last night, and I have seen him twice this morning and he is doing well.' Not surprising, considering the care he was receiving!

If you can't visit, send a note at least. A businessman of about 50 years of age, together with his wife, got saved one night during a series of my meetings. One night soon after I noticed he was not there so I wrote him a note telling him I was praying for him. The next night he was present and told how he had been greatly tempted, but that note helped him get through. He became a good soldier.

2. They should he encouraged to read their Bible daily, together with other good books. When I was a captain in Boston I went to the Bible Society and got inexpensive New Testaments, and I would give one to each convert, writing his or her name inside. Years after, I was visiting a corps. A young man asked me if I remembered him. I did not. He pulled out a little, well-worn Testament, pointed to his name and asked if I knew that writing. I did. He said, 'You gave me this New Testament years ago in Boston. I have kept it and read it ever since, and tonight I am being sworn in as a Salvation Army soldier.'

3. They must be taught to pray. Your new Christians need to be urged to make prayer regular and frequent. Teach them. Ask them about their prayer life. Pray with them.

4. They must be instructed to see the difference between sin and temptation. The devil will try to discourage them, making them think his temptations are sins, and proof no change has taken place in their hearts. Warn them they will certainly be tempted, but not to worry about that.

5. They should be encouraged to work for the salvation of others, especially for their own family and friends. 'Andrew found his own brother Simon, and he brought him to Jesus,' (John 1:42) the Bible says, and our converts must do likewise. Encourage them to give their witness, first to people close to them.

6. They should be led into the experience of being filled with the Spirit of love. They must not be allowed to stop at consecration, but must be pressed on into a definite experience of full salvation.

(*The Soul-Winners Secret*)

Stay healthy

The man who never relaxes, however religious he may be, is likely to become morose, irritable, and impatient. My wife tells me that when I get very tired, I become anxious for my children, gloomy and intense. And its then I begin to feel I must work more or pray longer. In those times she advises me to take some rest. I need to put on the brakes and rest by sheer force of will, if need be.

It is vital that the servant of God live a healthy life. That means he or she will relax. I know of evangelists who saw tremendous fruit for God in their early years, but then their health broke down and they had to pull back. I am convinced that if they had obeyed the Lord's rule of six days work and one day's rest, they would have kept going. Work is absolutely necessary for health, but so is rest.

A servant of God must also get enough sleep. I have heard General Booth say that he needed at least eight hours sleep a night. John Wesley could get along with six hours' sleep at night, though he had the happy faculty of taking naps through the day—even on horseback. No rule can be laid down, but we must each work out what we need, then do it for God.

Stay healthy, and use what health you have to love God and people.

(*The Soul-Winners Secret*)

Spiritual Formation Small Group Notes

Peter and Kerrie Farthing

Introduction

These are not regular small group Bible study notes. They include exercises and prayers to help you grow more like Jesus.

We strongly urge every group member to use a journal for the weeks you are doing these studies. Bring your journal to the small group, and use it at home. Write down anything that strikes you as you read Brengle's book. If you think God is talking to you about anything, write that down too. You could try praying by writing your prayers. You could list areas of your life you want God to help you with. Ask God to bring to your attention things he wants to change.

Frequently the notes will ask you to read a chapter from Brengle, or a portion of the Bible. We suggest in both instances you read out loud.

Most of the small group sessions will include some follow up on the week past and the previous group. We encourage you to agree on confidentiality, then be as open as you can.

Lots of sessions have prayer at the end. Your leader will guide you through the suggested approach to prayer.

Finally, for each week we suggest simple exercises to try at home. By practicing these follow-through exercises you will be giving the Holy Spirit extra opportunities to shape your life.

God bless you. Enjoy.

Peter and Kerrie

The Atonement

1. Can you describe one person you have known, or known about, who was genuinely compassionate?

2. Jesus told the story of the Good Samaritan who stopped to help the wounded traveller. Is there any person you should be stopping for more at the moment?

LEARN

3. Read together 'The Atonement (Part 1)'

a. Read Romans 8:5-8.

'Sin is a state of the heart.' What do you think this means?

b. 'Sin is a wrong *against God*?' Brengle gave examples from the lives of David and Joseph. How would you explain this truth, that our sin is against God?

4. Read 'The Atonement (Part 2)'

Brengle asked: 'How could God's love and holiness harmonise to secure mercy for the sinner and judgment against the sin?' In your own words, explain the dilemma God faced.

5. Read 'The Atonement (Part 3)'

Read Romans 3:23-26; Romans 5:6-8

What does the Bible teach us here about the atonement?

6. 'The death of Jesus is not a means of appeasing a Father who is unable or unwilling to forgive. It is the divinely appointed way by which sinners, who would otherwise face the wrath and judgment of God, can approach him and claim his mercy on the grounds that Christ bore that judgment by dying for them' (I Howard Marshall). What do you believe this truth means for your life?

 APPLY

7. God's atoning work has many practical implications for our lives. As a group, name as many as you can think of.

PRAY

Join together in prayers of praise and thanks to God for his atoning work in Christ.

We all know people who have not received God's pardon through the Cross of Christ. See if each member can name one person he or she would like to pray for. Go around the group saying who your person is. Then return to prayer and pray for each one by name.

FOLLOW-THROUGH

When you are alone, make a cross. Use material from your house or your garden—use whatever you like. Be simple or be creative—its up to you. Then place the cross in a strategic place, where you will see it often during the week—on your desk or in your car or at the place where you say your prayers.

When you see it, praise God for his atoning work in Jesus Christ. Thank him.

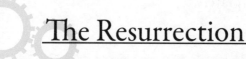

The Resurrection

 SHARE

1. Read together 'Witnesses to the resurrection.'

If somebody asked you, 'Are you a witness to the resurrection?' how would you answer? How would you explain your perspective?

2. Share on two things:

First, any feedback on your experience with the cross you made.

Second, any difficulties of any kind you have faced this past week.

REFLECT

3. Read 'Resurrection power.' What personal impact do you think Jesus' resurrection would have had on the disciples?

LEARN

4. 'His unique identity as Son of God was shown by the Spirit when Jesus was raised from the dead, setting him apart as the Messiah, our Master' (Romans 1:4 TM).

On the Day of Pentecost Peter told the assembled Jerusalem crowd: 'God untied the death ropes and raised him up. Death was no match for him ... There's no longer room for doubt—God made him Master and Messiah, this Jesus whom you killed on a cross' (Acts 2:24; 36 TM).

How do you think the resurrection proved that Jesus was the Christ, the Son of God?

5. How do you think Christ's resurrection proves that his atoning work is finished?

6. 'Christ has been raised to life! And he makes us certain that others will also be raised to life' (1 Corinthians 15:20 CEV). How would you explain, that 'he has become the very first to rise of all who sleep the sleep of death' (JBP)?.

7. Brengle tells a story about a young minister who was not practicing the resurrection life Christ had given him. What differences does the resurrection life of Christ *in us* make?

PRAY

Pray for each other, one by one, going around the group. Ask that the risen Christ would be known more, and that his power would continue to transform each person.

FOLLOW-THROUGH

There are two suggested exercises for this week.

1. If you have access to the internet, search for a picture of the resurrection which speaks to you. Print it off if you

can, and keep it with you when you say your prayers. Or bring it up on screen every day.

2. Write in your journal a one sentence prayer in which you thank God for all he achieved by raising Christ from the dead. Every day this week, pray that prayer.

The Holy Spirit

 SHARE

1. In recent weeks the group has looked at Christ's atonement and his resurrection. Share any follow-up thoughts, insights or questions you have had since those group meetings.

2. How are you finding the journaling? Each one share.

REFLECT

3. Read 'Who is the Holy Spirit? (Part 1)'

Brengle explains that the Holy Spirit is a person. Can you think of an example from your own life when the personality of the Holy Spirit has been obvious—that is, you have known him as a person?

4. Brengle also explains that the Holy Spirit is a presence. Can you think of any other examples from the Bible when the presence of God was experienced?

5. In your everyday living these days, where and how are you aware of the presence of the Holy Spirit?

6. Read 'Who is the Holy Spirit (Part 2).'

Read also John 14:1-21.

Each person share one sentence or phrase from John which strikes you as significant or important.

7. Brengle asked: 'Have you learnt to walk in the enabling power of the Spirit of God?' How would you describe the enabling impact the Spirit may have? Is there a personal story you would like to tell?

PRAY

Take some time to sit quietly, and wait for God.

1. First, offer a short and simple prayer, asking the Holy

Spirit to come, to be at work in your group and in your lives.

2. Then sit quietly, eyes closed, thinking about Jesus. You might like to imagine one favourite incident from Jesus' life. Take your time with this, don't rush.

3. Now ask the Holy Spirit to do what he does so well. For example:

- show you more of Christ,

- empower you

- clean you

- comfort you

- lead you

- grow his fruit in you.

4. Finally, thank him.

FOLLOW-THROUGH

This week we have two very simple exercises.

1. Find a song which is a prayer for the Holy Spirit to work in your life. Every day, listen to that song, or sing it or read the lyrics prayerfully.

2. Try this simple prayer exercise, known as 'spiritual breathing.'

When we breathe out we exhale the impure air. When we breathe in, we inhale pure air, rich in oxygen. Spiritual breathing is much the same: we breathe out our sins and breathe in the Holy Spirit.

(Note, once the Holy Spirit comes to live in a person, he does not leave every time the person sins. In this exercise we are not asking the Spirit to return. We are just using it symbolically to help us stay open to the Spirit.)

Exhale: that is, confess your sins. Thank God for forgiving you. (1 John 1:9).

Inhale: Open your life to the Spirit of God. Thank him that he lives in you. Ask him to fill every part of you today. (Ephesians 5:18).

Try praying this way every day.

Holiness

SHARE

1. What is the funniest movie you have ever seen? When did you laugh the most?

2. Last session we studied the Holy Spirit. We also prayed, asking the Holy Spirit to work in and through us. Do you have any thoughts or experiences to share by way of follow up?

LEARN

3. Read 'What is holiness?'

Brengle says, 'It is, in our measure, to be made like God. It is to be made a "participant of the Divine nature" (2 Peter 1:4) . . . Holiness, then, is conformity to the nature of God. It is likeness to God, as he is revealed in Jesus.'

How would you explain this?

4. How would you express the truth that God gives us some of his own nature so that we may live like him?

5. Read 'Why should I be holy?'

Each person share any truth from the Bible in that reading, which strikes you as important.

6. Read 'You don't need more power.'

How would you put in your own words what Brengle is explaining here?

 REFLECT

7. How could you apply all this in your life over the coming week. Try to personalise it.

8. Finish this sentence: 'If God made me a little more like Jesus, I would ....'

For example, 'If God made me a little more like Jesus, I'd be more patient at home.'

PRAY

One person can take responsibility for guiding the prayers. He or she will suggest each step below, giving time after each, for one or more people to pray.

1. Thank God for his Spirit's power already in your life, if you have received Christ.

2. Admit your need for holiness.

3. Open your life to his influence.

4. Ask God to grow his own nature in you.

Take your journal. Ask the Lord, 'Is there something you want to change in me, so that Christ is seen more in me?' If you get an idea of what he would like to change, write that down in your journal.

FOLLOW-THROUGH

Read Galatians 5:13-26.

1. Now read verses 22 and 23 and this time insert the word 'Jesus'. So it will be, 'Jesus is love, Jesus is joy, Jesus is peace . . . .' Think about this.

2. In your journal, write down each of the fruit of the Spirit one under the other

Love

Joy

Peace

Patience

. . . and so on.

Beside each one, make notes on what fruit God had produced in you so far. For example, has he given you more patience?

Highlight one or two 'fruit areas' where you think God might like to grow more. Write out a prayer, asking him to grow his nature in you. Make a note of any specific steps you need to take.

Christian Conversation

 SHARE

1. Each member tell the group about one interesting person you have spoken with.

2. Last session we looked at holiness. How did you go this past week in letting God transform you?

REFLECT

3. From what you have read in the Gospels, discuss Jesus' conversation. What do you think it would have been like?

4. Read James 3:3-10. What do you think is the main thing James was saying?

LEARN

5. Read 'Christian conversation' (76).

How do you respond to Brengle's statement: 'It is wrong to go on about the faults and weaknesses of others'?

6. Can you think of other kinds of conversation which are either wrong or unhelpful?

7. Brengle lists five people we hurt when we engage in sinful talk. Do you agree with him?

8. Read 'The remedy for sinful talk' (79) and 'Discipline your talk' (87).

Which suggestion do you personally find most helpful?

 **PRAY**

Once again, the group needs a leader at this point who will read out the prayer guidelines.

1. First of all, let's all be quiet before the Lord.

2. Now let's praise and thank the Lord.

3. Next, we are going to have a time of quiet confession. Each of us will now confess his/her sins quietly to God. Especially think of sins of conversation which you need to confess.

4. Out loud now, let's have some prayers, asking the Lord to make us more like Christ.

5. Finally, let's bring to God any special prayer concerns we have, or know about, at present.

 FOLLOW-THROUGH

Once again there are two follow-through exercises for this week.

1. Over the next few days, make a conscious effort to speak positively about people and to not do any negative talk at all.

2. In prayer, have a conversation with Jesus. Write this conversation down in your journal. Write it like a movie script, so you have what you say, then what Jesus says.

- Begin by asking Jesus to speak to you.
- Listen for how he might answer.
- Then write down, 'Jesus, I'm concerned about . . . What should I do?'
- Listen for his reply, and write it down.
- Continue the conversation until it is over.